Blood Revenge in Irregular Warfare

This book offers an original assessment of the ways in which the sociocultural code of blood revenge and its modern remnants shape irregular warfare.

Despite being a common driver of communal violence, blood revenge has received little attention from scholars. With many civil wars and insurgencies occurring in areas where the custom lingers, strengthening our understanding of blood revenge is essential for discerning how conflicts change and evolve. Drawing upon extensive multidisciplinary evidence, this book is the first in the literature on civil war and insurgency to analyse the impact of blood revenge and its modern remnants on irregular warfare. Even when blood revenge undergoes erosion, its unregulated version still shapes the social fabric of insurgency, although in different ways than its institutionalised counterpart. At times of political instability, the presence of a culture of retaliation weighs heavily on the dynamics of violent mobilisation, target selection, recruitment, and disengagement. This book brings in evidence from dozens of conflicts, providing unprecedented insights into how a better understanding of blood revenge can improve military blueprints for irregular warfare.

This book will be of much interest to students of insurgency, terrorism, military and strategic studies, anthropology, and sociology, as well as to decision-makers and irregular warfare professionals.

Roberto Colombo is a doctoral researcher in Central and East European Studies, University of Glasgow. He is the co-author of *Counterinsurgency Warfare and Brutalisation* (2021).

Emil A. Souleimanov is a full professor at the Department of Security Studies, Institute of Political Studies, Faculty of Social Sciences, Charles University. He is the author of *Understanding Ethnopolitical Conflict* (2013) and the co-author of *Counterinsurgency Warfare and Brutalisation* (2021).

Blood Revenge in Irregular Warfare

Causes and Consequences of a
Lingering Custom

**Roberto Colombo and
Emil A. Souleimanov**

Routledge
Taylor & Francis Group

LONDON AND NEW YORK

First published 2023
by Routledge
4 Park Square, Milton Park, Abingdon, Oxon OX14 4RN

and by Routledge
605 Third Avenue, New York, NY 10158

Routledge is an imprint of the Taylor & Francis Group, an informa business

British Library Cataloguing-in-Publication Data
A catalogue record for this book is available from the British Library

Library of Congress Cataloging-in-Publication Data
Names: Colombo, Roberto, 1996– author. | Souleimanov, Emil, author.
Title: Blood revenge in irregular warfare : causes and consequences of a
lingering custom / Roberto Colombo and Emil A. Souleimanov.
Description: Abingdon, Oxon ; New York, NY : Routledge, 2023. |
Includes bibliographical references. |
Identifiers: LCCN 2022056693 (print) | LCCN 2022056694 (ebook) |
ISBN 9781032481227 (hardback) | ISBN 9781032481241 (paperback) |
ISBN 9781003387527 (ebook)
Subjects: LCSH: Vendetta. | Irregular warfare. | Civil war. |
War and society.
Classification: LCC GN495 .C65 2023 (print) |
LCC GN495 (ebook) | DDC 303.6/6–dc23/eng/20230213
LC record available at https://lccn.loc.gov/2022056693
LC ebook record available at https://lccn.loc.gov/2022056694

ISBN: 978-1-032-48122-7 (hbk)
ISBN: 978-1-032-48124-1 (pbk)
ISBN: 978-1-003-38752-7 (ebk)

DOI: 10.4324/9781003387527

Typeset in Bembo
by Newgen Publishing UK

Contents

Acknowledgements

Research on the present manuscript was enabled by a research grant provided by the Grant Agency of the Czech Republic 21–14872S: "Fratricidal defection: How blood revenge shapes anti-jihadist mobilisation."

Abbreviations

AFL	Armed Forces of Liberia
ANA	Afghan National Army
AQAP	Al-Qaeda in the Arabian Peninsula
AQI	Al-Qaeda in Iraq
BRA	Bougainville Revolutionary Army
BRF	Bougainville Resistance Force
FLNC	National Liberation Front of Corsica
FM 3–24	Field Manual 3–24
FSA	Free Syrian Army
IFM	Isatabu Freedom Movement
IS	Islamic State
JKBW	Jaysh Khalid bin al-Waleed
MEF	Malaita Eagle Force
MILF	Moro Islamic Liberation Front
MNLF	Moro National Liberation Front
NPFL	National Patriotic Front of Liberia
PKK	Kurdistan Workers' Party
PNGDF	Papua New Guinea Defence Forces
TTP	Tehrik-E Taliban Pakistan

1 Introduction

Once a widespread custom across the globe, blood revenge never ceased captivating the interest of scholars and non-specialists alike. Popularised in TV broadcasts, episodes of blood revenge are often reported as sensational displays of a fading tradition. In 2019, during a popular Italian TV programme, the father of an Albanian man killed in 2015 by a retired elderly explained how the laws of the Italian state were meaningless in front of the custom of Albanian blood revenge, known as Kanun:

> Francesco ... the Italian state acquitted you, and you think you are safe. But I will find you: you can hide underground; you might even consider hiring bodyguards. But [rest assured that] me, my kinsmen, or even an assassin will find you and kill you.
>
> (Taviani 2019)

It comes as no surprise that the literature on blood revenge is both voluminous and rich in content. Anthropologists thoroughly explored the origins and evolutions of customary laws (Boehm 2011; MacCormack 1973), describing blood revenge as either a mechanism of stability (Gluckman 1955; White 2016) or an agency of disorder (Bloch 1962: 128). While ethnographers traced the residual vestiges of blood revenge in modern societies (Meçe 2017; Jalabadze 2012), military operations waged across the Middle East, North Caucasus, and South-East Asia incentivised scholars of security studies to better understand how blood revenge shapes conflicts taking place in "cultures of honour,"—that is, cultures "in which a person (usually a man) feels obliged to protect his or her reputation by answering insults, affronts, and threats, oftentimes through the use of violence" (Kilcullen 2009; Souleimanov & Aliyev 2015a; Cohen 2007: 212). Likewise, several studies have illustrated how blood revenge defines the patterns of inter-communal (Pendle 2018; Lee 2007), intra-communal

DOI: 10.4324/9781003387527-1

(Beckerman et al. 2009; Heyne 2007), and rebel violence (Souleimanov & Aliyev 2017; Kilcullen 2009).

Given the sustained academic interest in blood revenge, the dearth of studies tracing this customary code's decline, and its impact on the dynamics of irregular warfare, is rather puzzling. This observation should not mislead the reader into believing that previous research has not touched upon this phenomenon. In fact, several authors described the dissolution of blood revenge, as done so by Davies (1969) in his account of the uprooting of blood feuds in southwest England during the 13th century and Mills (1976) in his study on the outlawing of *Kataki-uchi* in pre-modern Japan. Nonetheless, discussion related to the erosion of this custom remains circumscribed to anthropological research, taking a rather marginal place in the political science literature.

To date, only a handful of studies have shed light on the impact of blood revenge on the dynamics of civil wars and insurgencies. In their pioneering study on the role of blood revenge as a pro-insurgent mobilising factor during the Russian-Chechen Wars of 1994–1996 and 1999–2009, Souleimanov and Aliyev (2015a) found that the compelling desire to avenge a fallen kinsmen killed by Russian troops pushed hundreds of apolitical Chechens to join rebel bands and engage in armed hostilities. In a separate study, the authors argue that sociocultural codes, including blood revenge, create an "asymmetry of values" between honorific rebels and institutionalised incumbents in favour of the former, which gain access to "mechanisms of violent mobilisation and support structures" largely unavailable to non-indigenous troops (Souleimanov & Aliyev 2015b: 679). More recently, Souleimanov et al. (2022a) produced the first comprehensive systematisation of the ways in which blood revenge shapes irregular warfare. Drawing upon multidisciplinary scholarship, cross-case qualitative evidence, and a quantitative dataset, the authors demonstrate that blood revenge denies avengers the possibility of free-riding on their social obligation of participating in the hostilities to seek vengeance, thus providing insurgent groups with a cost-effective solution to the collective action problem faced by belligerents in irregular conflicts. Nonetheless, gaps remain in our understanding of how blood revenge shapes civil wars and insurgencies, specifically regarding the regions in which sociocultural codes are yielding in favour of unregulated retaliatory practices resting upon socially sanctioned concepts of honour and revenge.

To fill this gap in the literature, this book spells out the key attributes of blood revenge, illustrates the causal mechanisms engendering its erosion, and maps its impact over the course of civil wars and insurgencies. This book reveals that blood revenge declines following a multi-staged process. First, the government centralises the judicial apparatus, providing individuals with a non-violent means for settling interpersonal disputes. Second, blood revenge is criminalised to deter people from recurring to self-made justice. Third, processes of societal modernisation erode the culture of honour upon which the logic of blood revenge rests. Fourth, the population comes to consider the recourse to blood revenge disdainful. For customary codes to disappear, both processes of state centralisation and societal rejection of the principle of kinship-centred vengeance must come to fruition. When the process of state centralisation is interrupted, such as when a country descends into civil war, local communities can experience a resurgence of blood revenge killings. Where the process of state centralisation is successful, but society does not relinquish traditional values, a culture of retaliation may outlast the authority's suppressive efforts. This is the case of communities caught amid a civil war, which relinquish the state authority in favour of traditional conflict resolution mechanisms based on customary codes.

By shedding light on the complexity of this long-lasting process, this book demonstrates that blood revenge is a resilient custom holding crucial relevance for understanding patterns of violence and restraint in irregular conflicts. Specifically, we find that even in modern societies, the decline of blood revenge has not led to the complete disappearance of revenge-seeking practices. In areas where concepts of male honour and warrior ethos outlast the erosion of blood revenge, people may still seek to respond to insults and humiliations through the act of violent mobilisation. This societal condition, defined in this book as a "culture of retaliation," drives avengers to eschew neutrality and participate in irregular conflicts. No longer bound to the tightly regulated mechanisms of blood revenge, individuals are largely left free to decide when an insult is worthy of retaliation, how the retaliatory attack is to be carried out, and who fits the profile of a viable target. In contrast to areas in which blood revenge endures, where tribesmen are compelled to mobilise due to apolitical motives, avengers who adhere to a loose culture of retaliation may find in political, religious, or economic grievances, the trigger for revenge-driven violent mobilisation. The increase in potential triggers of violent mobilisation translates, in turn, to higher numbers of avengers seeking membership in armed groups and taking part in high-risk collective action.

These avengers may not necessarily strike against the direct culprit or his close relatives, who typically cease being considered as legitimate targets due to the weakening of kinship ties, but rather decide to randomly select anyone belonging to the "guilty" community as a suitable victim. The erosion of the selectivity principles regulating institutionalised forms of blood revenge puts entire (sub)ethnic, (sub)religious, or (sub)cultural groups in danger, thus contributing to scaling up the figures of people exposed to the risk of retaliatory attacks. For armed actors, the presence of individuals seeking to restore their honour offers important opportunities for recruiting and retaining a pool of highly determined volunteers unlikely to free-ride on high-risk collective action. Once recruited, avengers are often progressively indoctrinated and encouraged to keep fighting in pursuit of the group's ideological aims. With notions of individual and collective honour enduring amongst societies undergoing a process of modernisation, the logic of retaliation killings as a reputation-restoring practice is likely to persist—even if outside the boundaries of what is ethically, legally, and morally accepted by society at large.

Such dynamics can have far-reaching consequences for civil and military practitioners involved in counter-insurgency, stability, and peace-keeping operations, especially because blood revenge—or its modern remnants—influences key dynamics in irregular conflicts, including the patterns of violent mobilisation, target selection, recruitment, and disengagement. In support of this argument, we draw from an extensive overview of empirical evidence produced by anthropologists, ethnographers, historians, and experts of security studies to illustrate the functioning of the mechanism supporting the decline of blood revenge and its impact over the course of irregular conflicts.

Aims and Scope

Once confined to the realm of military and colonial history, the interest in sociocultural intelligence, defined as "intelligence related to culture, belief, morals, law, customs and habits acquired by humans as members of society," came roaring back in the wake of the U.S. intervention in Afghanistan and Iraq (Yalçinkaya & Özer 2017: 439). Trained and equipped to fight high-intensity conflicts against conventional enemies, the coalition forces were experiencing difficulties in fighting elusive insurgencies that they did not understand. As testified by a U.S. commander deployed in Iraq,

> I had perfect situational awareness. What I lacked was cultural awareness. I knew where every enemy tank was dug in on the outskirts of Tallil. Only problem was, my soldiers had to fight fanatics charging on foot or in pickups and firing AK-47s and RPGs [rocket-propelled grenades]. Great technical intelligence. Wrong enemy.
>
> (McFate 2005a: 25)

To overcome the obstacles posed by the lack of sociocultural understanding, the doctrines underpinning the conduct of counterinsurgency operations received a substantial overhaul aimed at maximising the troops' capability to operate in foreign, unfamiliar environments. Accordingly, the latest version of the U.S. *Field Manual 3–24: Insurgencies and Countering Insurgencies* (hereinafter FM 3–24) dedicates an entire chapter to culture, in which the emphasis is placed on warning soldiers against the perils of neglecting sociocultural customs: "If Soldiers and Marines assume that the local population will perceive actions the way that they do, they are likely to misjudge their reactions" (U.S. Government 2014: 3–1). The consequences of ignoring culture when countering insurgencies are made explicit by McFate, an anthropologist who greatly contributed to the drafting of the latest FM 3–24:

> Misunderstanding culture at a strategic level can produce policies that exacerbate an insurgency; a lack of cultural knowledge at an operational level can lead to negative public opinion; and ignorance of the culture at a tactical level endangers both civilians and troops.
>
> (McFate, 2005b: 43)

With the appetite for sociocultural intelligence becoming a pressing need of military and intelligence professionals, efforts aimed at reinforcing the collective understanding of how sociocultural codes shape irregular warfare assumes a role of primary importance. This holds especially true for areas in which modernisation processes are shaping the context and character of society. With the pace of megatrends such as population growth and urbanisation accelerating globally, many countries are likely to undergo profound changes in their customs and habits, with direct consequences for military and civil professionals working to counter the combined threats of insurgency, terrorism, and ethno-sectarian warfare (Kilcullen 2013: 28).

Diving deep into this largely uncharted research area, this book is the first to analyse the ways in which the remnants of the sociocultural code of retaliation, also known as "blood revenge," shape the dynamics of irregular warfare in societies where traditional customs are eroding. To account for the fluidity and complexity of the processes that drive change in modern societies, the book roots its findings on an extensive review of anthropological, ethnographic, historical, and sociological literature discussing the rise and decline of blood revenge. Adopting an interdisciplinary approach to the study of violence, the central chapters show that the erosion of blood revenge is rarely if ever a linear process, which is often interrupted or reversed at times of crisis and political instability. Without a robust appreciation of the shifting attitudes, customs, and beliefs of the local population, policymakers and military professionals can hardly achieve that "exceptional ability to understand people, their culture and their motivation" necessary to operate in culturally distant environments (Scales 2007: 1).

In addressing this growing need for sociocultural knowledge, this book not only investigates the ways in which blood revenge and retaliatory practices drive conflict but also underscores how traditional conflict resolution mechanisms can be exploited to bring stability in war-torn communities. Furthermore, it provides valuable insights into how the tools of state power can be fully leveraged to address local grievances and prevent conflict. To make an example, doctrinal axioms such as "money can be more important than ammunition" would find more concrete meaning if implemented as part of systematic engagements with local tribes aimed at de-escalating conflict using traditional conflict resolutions mechanisms (Petraeus 2006: 47). Accordingly, Chapter 5 concludes by providing a list of actionable takeaways for civil and military practitioners deployed in areas where concepts of honour and revenge regulate the everyday lives of local communities. In doing so, this book adopts a policy-oriented approach to research, aimed at improving existing blueprints for irregular warfare without losing sight of the moral and ethical principles underpinning the conduct of modern counter-insurgency (U.S. Government 2014, Chapter 13, p. 1).

Data and Methods

To fully appreciate the relevance of blood revenge in irregular warfare, this book brings in evidence from dozens of different ethnic, religious, and political actors involved in armed conflicts across Asia, Africa, Europe, Oceania, the Middle East, and the Caucasus regions. In doing so, the book marks a departure from previous studies, largely reliant upon single case study approaches, to cast a far wider empirical net and provide a more comprehensive picture of the role of blood revenge in civil war (Souleimanov & Aliyev 2015a; Hinton 1998; Boyle 2010). This approach, which rests upon a consolidated tradition of cross-case research in the field of security studies, contributes to highlighting recurrent patterns in the data collected from different empirical settings without losing analytical rigour or compromising the generalisability of the book's main findings.

The empirical contribution to the existing literature is significant if one considers that aggregate data on the role of blood revenge in irregular warfare is, with a few exceptions, largely non-existent.[1] Many individuals who live in societies with strong concepts of honour and retaliation are often reluctant to share information on episodes of blood revenge with outsiders, especially because perpetrators typically face charges of voluntary manslaughter heavily criminalised under the state penal code.[2] To make an example, a research group found that, across the islands of Papua New Guinea, investigative reporting on episodes of crime and violence is very low "not because it is banned or restricted, but because reporters and like-minded people are fearful of 'payback' or revenge attacks" (BTI 2016: 9). In addition, the widespread misuse in international press articles and journalistic accounts of terms such as "blood revenge" and "blood feud" further complicates the collection of reliable data, which must be manually filtered and vetted in accordance with the main anthropological features of blood revenge provided in Chapter 2.

This effort, aimed at retrieving reliable data from disaggregated open-source information, constitutes a valuable framework of reference for scholars who are seeking to strengthen our understanding of the logic of violence in irregular conflicts. In collating knowledge taken from a wide array of diverse sources, this book sets the initial empirical foundations necessary to identify suitable cases for in-depth inquiries into important, yet so far overlooked aspects of civil wars and insurgencies.

Contents

This book consists of an introduction, four central chapters, and a conclusion. This introductory chapter spelt out the book's main aims and offered an overview of the data and methods employed in the core chapters. Situating the study of blood revenge at the intersection between anthropology and political science, this chapter demonstrates the importance of strengthening the collective understanding of how sociocultural codes shape the inception, course, and aftermath of irregular conflicts.

Chapter 2 conceptualises the main features of blood revenge, including its role as a conflict resolution mechanism. Drawing upon an in-depth review of anthropological and ethnographic studies from across the globe, the chapter traces the origins and social function of this age-old custom, provides an in-depth discussion of its key features, and illustrates how its presence shapes inter-communal and intra-communal violence. It shows that the severe social sanctions suffered by failed avengers play an important role in the violent mobilisation of kinsmen seeking to restore their stained reputation. This chapter introduces scholars of security studies to largely understudied, yet crucially relevant cultural practices of many countries affected by conflict and political instability.

Chapter 3 offers an in-depth scrutiny of the causal pathways leading to the erosion of blood revenge. It discusses the emergence of a centralised judicial apparatus, the criminalisation of blood revenge, the downfall of the culture of honour, and the development of a key sociological trait of contemporary society, which we define as "the self-controlling individual." Drawing upon dozens of past and present cases from across the globe, the chapter offers an original summary of the existing anthropological and sociological material describing the long-lasting decline of blood revenge and its effects on the traits of inter-communal, intra-communal, and insurgent violence. A stronger understanding of the societal dynamics leading to the erosion of blood revenge sets the contextual ground necessary to discern the effects of these processes over the inception, course, and aftermath of irregular conflicts.

Chapter 4 provides a comprehensive account of the ways in which blood revenge shapes irregular warfare. After situating the study of blood revenge in the political science literature, the chapter outlines the strong relevance of this embedded sociocultural code for understanding the key aspects of irregular conflicts, including the patterns of violent mobilisation, target selection, recruitment, and disengagement. It brings in evidence from a wide array of conflict zones, illustrating the cross-case relevance of blood revenge on largely overlooked aspects of insurgencies, civil wars, and asymmetric conflicts.

Chapter 5 investigates the role of blood revenge in irregular conflicts taking place in societies undergoing a process of state centralisation or societal rejection of customary codes. It derives contextual insights from Chapter 3 to explain why, when, and how the culture of retaliation flares up at times of civil war and political instability. Drawing upon a robust overview of empirical evidence from recent global conflicts, this chapter shows how a relatively weak or subsided customary code—or its modern remnants—can resurface and shape the dynamics of irregular conflicts. It concludes by advancing three main takeaways for law enforcement agencies, civil servants, and military practitioners seeking to improve their performances in conflict and post-conflict operations.

The book's main findings are summarised and tied together in Chapter 6, which offers additional avenues for further research into the logic of blood revenge in irregular warfare. It argues that blood revenge and its modern remnants constitute key drivers of violence in irregular conflicts, whilst stressing that traditional conflict resolution mechanisms represent important tools for de-escalating conflicts and preventing the diffusion of violent extremism. The chapter calls for future research into a long-ignored, yet crucially relevant aspect of civil wars and insurgencies, which warrants more attention from the community of irregular warfare professionals.

Notes

1 Although blood revenge is occasionally mentioned as an important driver of violence in civil wars and insurgencies, only a handful of academic studies analytically address the ways in which blood revenge shapes irregular warfare. These include, among others, the works of Souleimanov and Aliyev (2015a, 2015b, 2017), Ratelle and Souleimanov (2017), and Souleimanov et al. (2022a), which are discussed in Chapter 4.
2 In Yemen, for instance, the Law of Crimes and Punishment No. 12 of 1994 assigns the penalty of capital punishment to individuals guilty of having performed a blood revenge murder (Government of Yemen, 1994). Similarly, the Albanian Criminal Code stipulates that "murder committed due [to] blood feud shall be punishable to not less than 30 years of life imprisonment" (ERALIUS 2015).

References

Beckerman, Stephen; Erickson, L. Pamela; Yost, James; Regalado, Jhanira; Jaramillo, Lilia; Sparks, Corey; Iromenga, Moises & Long, Kathryn. "Life Histories, Blood Revenge, and Reproductive Success among the Waorani of Ecuador," *PNAS* 106(20), 2009: 8134–8139. https://doi.org/10.1073/pnas.0901431106

Bloch, Marc. *Feudal Society I: The Growth of Ties of Dependence* (London: Routledge, 1962). ISBN-10: 0226059782.

Boehm, Christopher. "Retaliatory Violence in Human Prehistory," *The British Journal of Criminology* 51(3), 2011: 518–534. DOI: www.jstor.org/stable/23640324

Boyle, J. Michael. "Revenge and Reprisal Violence in Kosovo," *Conflict, Security & Development* 10(2), 2010: 189–216. DOI: 10.1080/14678801003665968

BTI. "Papua New Guinea: Country Report," *BTI Project*, 2016. Available at: https://bti-project.org/fileadmin/api/content/en/downloads/reports/country_report_2016_PNG.pdf

Cohen, Dov. "Culture of Honor" in *Encyclopaedia of Social Psychology I*, edited by Baumeister, Roy & Vohs, Kathleen (Thousand Oaks: SAGE Publications, 2007), 212–213. ISBN: 9781452265681.

Davies, Robert Rees. "The Survival of the Bloodfeud in Medieval Wales," *History* 54(182), 1969: 338–357. www.jstor.org/stable/24407103

ERALIUS. "Criminal Code of the Republic of Albania." 2015. Available at: www.warnathgroup.com/wp-content/uploads/2017/11/Albania_CC_1995_am2015_en.pdf

Gluckman, Max. "The Peace in the Feud," *Past & Present* 8, 1955: 1–14. www.jstor.org/stable/649774

Government of Yemen. "Republican Decree, By Law No. 12, 1994 Concerning Crimes and Penalties." 1994. Available at: https://wipolex-res.wipo.int/edocs/lexdocs/laws/en/ye/ye007en.pdf

Heyne, Georg. "Notes on Blood Revenge among the Reindeer Evenki of Manchuria (Northeast China)," *Asian Folklore Studies* 66(1/2), 2007: 165–178. www.jstor.org/stable/30030455

Hinton, L. Alexander. "A Head for an Eye: Revenge in the Cambodian Genocide," *American Ethnologist* 25(3), 1998: 352–377. www.jstor.org/stable/645789

Jalabadze, Natia. "The Resurgence of Blood Feud in the Georgian Lowlands," *Caucasus Analytical Digest* 42(30), 2012: 7–9. Available at: https://css.ethz.ch/content/dam/ethz/special-interest/gess/cis/center-for-securities-studies/pdfs/CAD-42-7-9.pdf

Kilcullen, David. *Out of the Mountains: The Coming Age of the Urban Guerrilla* (London: Hurst, 2013). ISBN: 978-0-19-973750-5.

Kilcullen, David. *The Accidental Guerrilla: Fighting Small Wars in the Midst of a Big One* (New York: Oxford University Press, 2009). ISBN-10: 9780199754090.

Lee, E. Wayne. "Peace Chiefs and Blood Revenge: Patterns of Restraint in Native American Warfare, 1500–1800," *The Journal of Military History* 71(3), 2007: 701–741. https://doi.org/10.1353/jmh.2007.0216

MacCormack, Geoffrey. "Revenge and Compensation in Early Law," *The American Journal of Comparative Law* 21(1), 1973: 69–85. https://doi.org/10.2307/839418

McFate, Montgomery. "Anthropology and Counterinsurgency: The Strange Story of Their Curious Relationship," *Military Review*, March–April 2005a. www.hsdl.org/?view&did=452717

McFate, Montgomery. "The Military Utility of Understanding Adversary Culture," *Joint Force Quarterly* 38, 2005b: 42–48. https://smallwarsjournal.com/documents/mcfate2.pdf

Meçe, Merita. "Living in Uncertainty: Resurgence of Blood Feud in Albanian Post-Socialist Society and Its Consequences on Children and Young Adults," *Contemporary Readings in Law and Social Justice* 9(2), 2017: 28–38. DOI: 10.22381/CRLSJ9220172

Mills, D. "Kataki-Uchi: The Practice of Blood-Revenge in Pre-Modern Japan," *Modern Asian Studies* 10(4), 1976: 525–542. DOI: www.jstor.org/stable/311761

Pendle, R. Naomi. "'The Dead Are Just to Drink from': Recycling Ideas of Revenge among the Western Dinka, South Sudan," *Africa* 88(1), 2018: 99–121. DOI: 10.1017/S0001972017000584

Petraeus, H. David. "Learning Counterinsurgency: Observations from Soldiering in Iraq," *Military Review*, January–February 2006: 2–12. www.armyupress.army.mil/Portals/7/military-review/COIN%20Reader/docs/Petraues_Learning_Counterinsurgency.pdf

Ratelle, Jean-François & Souleimanov, A. Emil. "Retaliation in Rebellion: The Missing Link to Explaining Insurgent Violence in Dagestan," *Terrorism and Political Violence* 29(4), 2017: 573–592. DOI: 10.1080/09546553.2015.1005076

Scales, H. Robert. "Statement for the Record," *Senate Armed Services Committee*, April 25, 2007. Available at: www.globalsecurity.org/military/library/congress/2007_hr/070425-scales.pdf

Souleimanov, A. Emil & Aliyev, Huseyn. "Blood Revenge and Violent Mobilization: Evidence from the Chechen Wars," *International Security* 40(2), 2015a: 158–180. DOI: 10.1162/ISEC_a_00219

Souleimanov, A. Emil & Aliyev, Huseyn. "Asymmetry of Values, Indigenous Forces, and Incumbent Success in Counterinsurgency: Evidence from Chechnya," *Journal of Strategic Studies* 38(5), 2015b: 678–703. https://doi.org/10.1080/0140239 0.2014.952409

Souleimanov, A. Emil & Aliyev, Huseyn. *How Socio-Cultural Codes Shaped Violent Mobilisation and Pro-insurgent Support in the Chechen Wars* (Cham: Palgrave Macmillan, 2017). ISBN-10: 3319529161

Souleimanov, A. Emil; Siroky, S. David & Colombo, Roberto. "Blood Revenge in Civil War: Proof-of-Concept," *Security Studies*, 2022a. DOI: 10.1080/09636412.2023.2153731.

Taviani, Giulia. "Dalla Kanun Albanese alla Mafia Italiana: La Vendetta Non Risparmia Nessuno," *Periodico Daily*, February 11, 2019. Available at: www.per iodicodaily.com/dalla-kanun-albanese-alla-mafia-italiana-la-vendetta-non-risparmia-nessuno/

U.S. Government. *FM 3–24 MCWP 3–33.5: Insurgencies and Countering Insurgencies* (Washington, DC: Department of the Army, 2014). Available at: https://irp.fas.org/doddir/army/fm3-24.pdf

White, Stephen. "'The Peace in the Feud' Revisited: Feuds in the Peace in Medieval European Feuds" in *Making Early Mediaeval Societies*, edited by Cooper, Conrad & Leyser, Kate (Cambridge: Cambridge Press, 2016), 220–243. ISBN: 9781107138803.

Yalçinkaya, Haldun & Özer, Yusuf. "Another Lesson Learned in Afghanistan: The Concept of Cultural Intelligence," *International Peacekeeping* 24(3), 2017: 439–460. DOI: 10.1080/13533312.2016.1244485

2 Conceptualising Blood Revenge

Often misconceived as a "bloodthirsty and anarchic" means of settling interpersonal disputes, blood revenge must be differentiated from revenge killings that occur when "a person has suffered a wrongdoing and therefore reacts emotionally against the [perceived] perpetrator" (Wood 2006: 88; Meier 2019: 6). When the causal pathway of revenge killing displays a "highly emotional content" and does not abide by the social norms regulating *blood* revenge murders, the act of killing loses its ritual function designed to terminate a conflict "by re-establishing the balance of honour and power" between two factions (Frijda & Mesquita 2000: 56; Kuschel 1993: 691). As seeking revenge "in search for emotional satisfaction" does not constitute an acceptable justification for a retaliatory murder under customary law, the utmost care should be placed on distinguishing between instances of revenge and *blood* revenge (Boyle 2010: 191). Failing to differentiate between the two would risk contaminating the data presented in support of case study research, negatively affecting the collective understanding of blood revenge and the dynamics leading to its decline and resurgence.

In his seminal work on the customary law of Yanomamo Indians, Chagnon (1988: 965) defined blood revenge as "a retaliatory killing in which the initial victim's close kinsmen conduct a revenge raid on the members of the current community of the initial killer." This implies that the initial culprit is not the only licit target of the offended individual or his male agnates. As any kinsmen on the culprit's patrilineal side is held responsible for his relative's wrongdoings on the lines that they both share the same *blood*, multiple individuals are eligible for a blood revenge killing regardless of whether they share a biological tie with the culprit. As explained by Reed and Segal (2011: 72), "much of the tribal genealogy is based on fictive kinship ties." Blood brothers, godparents, godchildren, and close family friends are all considered as a culprit's close relatives, and thus are all held equally responsible for the culprit's own misdeeds.

DOI: 10.4324/9781003387527-2

By omitting to specify the amount of time passing between the initial and the retaliatory murder, Chagnon (1988) underscored that blood revenge has no expiry date, as vengeance can be taken decades after the triggering event, often involving individuals with little or no knowledge of that episode. This is especially the case when the avenger is either forced to hunt down his designated target or when the sons of the murdered person are too young to carry out their revenge. While Mills (1976: 528) recorded a case of a man who dedicated more than 30 years of his life to tracking down his father's murderer in 19th-century Japan, Aggelis reported the pledge made by a pregnant woman in Crete to her murdered husband: "Don't worry/my beloved/ the one who will take revenge on you/ is now resting in my body" (cited in Tsantiropoulos 2008: 71). By the act of vengeance, members of the offender's kinship group (family, clan, or tribe) become "offended" and are required to exact revenge on the transgressor. According to Kuschel (1993: 691), blood revenge is "an act of avenging a previous murder in order to terminate a conflict by re-establishing the balance of honour and power." Thus, blood revenge has strong kinetic energy as it drags avengers on both sides into a vicious cycle of potentially never-ending violence, a condition known as "blood feud." With this definition of blood revenge in mind, we turn to examine the origins, social functions, and key features of this age-old custom.

Origins and Social Function of Blood Revenge

Why does blood revenge exist? As a form of self-help justice, this age-old customary code constitutes one of several unwritten rules of social conduct upheld across societies organised around notions of honour and revenge. Anthropologists and historians alike seem to agree that blood revenge, as an institutionalised sociocultural code, was initially developed as a "mechanism of social control" necessary to regulate communal life in societies lacking a central authority capable or willing to enforce its system of control upon the population (Waldmann 2001: 438; Gluckman 1955).

In this state of virtual anarchy, the availability of a socially sanctioned means to punish wrongdoers acts as a powerful deterrent against deviant behaviour. As explained by Barclay (1990: 128), in anarchic policies, a wound of honour is to be met with swift retaliation, so that "everyone becomes very much aware of the potential consequences of rash behaviour. Each person learns the need for self-restraint." In his account of the customary laws of the Franks, a Germanic-speaking people who inherited large swathes of the collapsed Western Roman Empire, Wallace-Hadrill (1959: 467) explained that it was the retaliatory component of blood revenge that urged each tribesman to settle disputes through non-violent means: "Without the sanction of blood, composition would have stood a poor chance in a world lacking not simply a police-force but any concept of public order." Similarly, in his monograph describing the social system of the Nuer tribes of the Greater Upper Nile region, Evans-Pritchard (1940: 150) explained that the dangers of falling victim to a retaliatory raid constituted "the most important legal sanction within a tribe and the main guarantee of an individual's life and property."

The deterrent function of blood revenge is endowed with credibility by the readiness of each kinsman to act on behalf of a relative who suffered an insult or severe injury. As argued by Halsall (1999: 8), blood revenge is a family affair, for it is the responsibility of each kinsman to enforce justice when no other policing entity can: "the threat of 'mutually assured destruction' of families through quite legitimate [cycles of] reciprocal killing, involving widely defined kin-groups, acted as a brake upon any urge to use lethal violence to settle disputes." With the social order of the group in traditional cultures of honour resting upon what Hobfoll (2018: 24) defined as the "biological" belonging of individuals to their community, the importance of preserving peace compels each member to recognise and enforce a series of reciprocal arrangements, based on a system of sanctions and rewards, to prevent the system from descending into lawlessness (Benson 1988).

In emphasising the strong regulatory potential of blood revenge killings, anthropologists underscore another crucial feature of communal life, namely the importance of defending one's reputation from the injuries and insults caused by others. In cultures of honour, a man must always be ready to seek retribution, even at the cost of his own life, because his family's dignity, integrity, and social status are dependent on it. Put differently, a family's security, wealth, and status can only grow insofar as its members preserve intact their respective reputation, in this way accumulating what can be considered as the "primary currency" of honour societies (McCabe 2011: 60). As specified by Pitt-Rivers (1965: 22, 24), "honour establishes status" and its achievement "depends upon the ability to silence anyone who would dispute the title." Ethnographic research carried out across a wide spectrum of societies confirms these considerations. In Northern Pakistan, families who fail to defend their honour display weakness and incentivise their neighbours to "push them out" of the competition for land, water, and women (Aase 2013: 14). Similarly, the indigenous tribesmen of Bellona, a remote island in the Solomon archipelago, are well aware that their status is contingent upon their ability to defend and retain honour. As found by Kuschel (1993: 704), most male agnates diligently avenge their deceased relatives, justifying their actions by explaining that "One-sidedness is bad … because it indicates cowardice."

Given that every kinsman is ready to wash off an insult with the blood of its perpetrator or one of his close relatives, the custom of blood revenge creates a balance of power within the group, ensuring that affronts to one's reputation will be followed by a swift retaliation in kind. This condition regulates the scope and character of violence, setting restrictions for when, where, and how blood revenge can be exacted. In his seminal volume on the role of blood revenge in the 19th-century tribal Montenegro, Boehm (1984) explained that the rules of blood revenge regulated the modalities and scope of retaliatory killings, thus preventing disputes from escalating to open warfare—a condition that tribesmen avoided in all but the most severe circumstances. As he put it, "feuds were dangerous, stressful, economically costly, and generally inconvenient from a practical standpoint" (Ibid.: 88). Accordingly, the death of a family member does not always demand retribution. In cases where the killer acted honourably, for instance, to protect a leader or a close kinsman, or when the slayed was engaging in dishonourable behaviour, such as stealing or carrying out an unsanctioned assassination, the latter's kinsmen would be prevented from rightfully invoking blood revenge (Rosenthal 1966: 135). In fact, an inappropriate use of violence by a member of the community may even prompt multiple agnates to turn their weapons against their relatives, thus releasing the injured party from the obligation of blood revenge. During his permanence with the Chukchee tribesmen, the indigenous people inhabiting a remote corner of Eastern Siberia, a 20th-century anthropologist was told how local tribesmen killed one of their own members to avoid triggering a blood feud with the injured party:

> [When a family member killed another tribesmen, the former's relatives decided to kill the culprit themselves] … "Otherwise," they said, "he will be killed by somebody else, and we shall have a feud on our hands." His own brother came to his camp, and, watching his opportunity, stabbed him in the back with a knife. This act was approved by the common consent of all the neighbours, because he was a bad one, a source of torment to the others.
>
> (Bagoras 1901: 631, cited in Czaplicka 1914: 25)

Often compared by scholars of strategic studies to the logic underpinning nuclear deterrence schemes, the highly credible threat of violent retaliation engenders a suppressive effect on the deviant behaviour by imposing potential costs that far outweigh any perceived benefit (Thrasher & Handfield 2018: 1960). In early modern societies, kings and rulers often recognised the important regulatory potential of blood revenge, integrating the custom within the wider set of legal options available for families seeking redress. This was the case in pre-modern Japan, where samurais were only allowed to seek vengeance if authorised by the central government authorities (Mills 1976). Similarly, in Mediaeval Iceland, avengers were given a specific amount of time to carry out a blood revenge killing. Once expired, blood revenge could no longer be taken and the injured party had to bring the case to the *Althing*, an assembly of *goðar* (landed freemen), which would take care of settling the dispute on the plaintiff's behalf (Perrin 2016: 148). In this way, blood revenge survived the transition from a state of virtual lawlessness to the rise and consolidation of organised systems of governance, finding its place in sets of legal codes that are still upheld by several governments across the globe up to this day.

Principles of Blood Revenge

After studying the customary laws of several Bedouin tribes, the 19th-century explorer Burckhardt (1831: 312) noted that "the fundamental laws of blood-revenge are the same, and universal throughout the whole Arabian desert." Burckhardt's observation constitutes an important reminder for the students of customary practices. Although the principles of blood revenge are consistent across societies practising institutionalised forms of self-help justice, blood revenge is a context-bound custom and researchers should expect to encounter variations within these principles when carrying out ethnographic research. In providing an overview of the principles underpinning blood revenge practices, we underscore that cross-case divergences do exist, and scholars should take extra care in reviewing the customary traditions of a given population before expounding their role in contexts of civil war and insurgency.

To be categorised as an act of blood revenge, a retaliatory attack must display four features. First, it must be performed by a *single individual* or a *group of close kinsmen*. When a war party is involved, a retaliatory killing bears the risk of escalating into open tribal warfare (Chagnon 1988). As reported by Lee (2014) in his study of indigenous American tribal customs, involving large groups in a quest of blood revenge can drag the entire tribe into undesired yet inescapable conflicts. After performing a blood revenge killing, a Cherokee tribesman stated: "if Catawbas [the culprit's tribe] continue to take Revenge, we will not only go against them Ourselves, but draw the whole People of our Nation against them" (Ibid.: 137). A more recent episode of blood revenge spiralled out of control occurred in 1963, when a detachment of Indian policemen deployed in the mountains of Eastern Himalaya, after siding with a clan involved in a local blood feud, was exterminated in an ambush by a tribal war party seeking to gain the upper hand against the opponent (Tamut 2019). Thus, collective killings cannot be considered blood revenge even though vengeance might be invoked as a pretext for triggering the hostilities between the two involved factions.

Second, as underscored by MacCormack (1973), blood revenge must be *reciprocal*, in the sense that unprovoked acts of violence cannot be considered instances of blood revenge. The concept of reciprocity is enshrined in the customary laws of traditional societies, as testified by some of the most iconic expressions of populations that for centuries have been practising blood revenge. While for Middle Eastern nomadic tribes "blood demands blood" (Cohen-Mor 2013: 50), Hinton (1998: 364) reports that, during the Khmer Rouge regime in Cambodia, government cadres would "shout at the top of their lungs: 'Blood avenges blood!'" to deter the population from engaging in anti-incumbent activity. Similarly, in Mediaeval Finland, an avenger would always seek to "recover" the blood of his dead kinsmen slayed by rival clans (Matikainen 2002), an expression that reiterates the Chechen saying, "Chechens never forgive blood" (Souleimanov & Aliyev 2015: 161).

Third, the target of a revenge killing must be chosen *selectively*. Traditionally, blood revenge can be accomplished—and one's honour restored—only when the avenger retaliates against either the perpetrator of the insult or one of his close male—and only male—relatives. Women, children, elderly, and disabled individuals are considered illegitimate targets of blood revenge attacks and killing them does not restore a man's honour: as such, these groups are usually exempt from retaliatory attacks. In contemporary Albania, for instance, the killing of women out of revenge is seen as a sign of cowardice and failure to follow the most sacred tenets of *Kanun*, the codified set of local customary practices (Rukaj 2012). As the customary codes upheld by Turkish tribesmen make clear, "a man must kill a man" for blood revenge to be accomplished (Tezcan 1982: 10).

Although women can neither partake in a blood revenge murder nor fall victim to one, the role that they traditionally play in such cases can still be important. In fact, women can pressure their menfolk into accomplishing a blood revenge murder as a way of restoring their wounded honour. Using the survey data collected from American college students living in regions where the culture of honour is still prominent, Barnes et al. (2012: 1020) find that men's militant responses to terrorist attacks are often endorsed by the female members of a given community: "women in honour cultures might pronounce such responses as right and good and call upon men to defend their country's good name from the insult of an attack." As reported by Robinson after visiting the tribal areas of Sudan in the 1920s, women can resort to multiple techniques to force their men to speed up the process of exacting blood revenge:

> A quarrel occurred between the Lahawiin and the Halawiin and a man of some standing was killed. The women of the Lahawiin thereupon wrapped up their right hands and forearms in raw hide rendering the limb useless and swore so to continue until they had been given the forearm of one of their tribal enemies ... [as this condition] hampered the women in the preparation of food and the performance of their household duties, the men were put to great inconvenience, and have considerable incentive to go and kill their enemy in order to have peace at home.
>
> (Robinson 1921: 107)

Similarly, in some parts of the world, class encroached on the practice of blood revenge. For example, a serf would not be able to declare blood revenge on a noble, and a peasant insulted by a noble would need to either ask for special permission to perform the murder or exact his vengeance on a person from an inferior class (Vaporis 2020: 240; Kaminsky 2002; Renteln 1988: 19).

Fourth, a blood revenge killing consists of an act of *equivalent* retaliation. As explained by Patton (1901: 708) in his study on the customary codes of Arabic tribes, the rule of blood revenge *(th'ar)* "is that an equivalent of the blood shed is to be obtained ... [while] in the blood-bath the aim is merely to satisfy the passion of the avengers" and therefore the retaliation stops being considered as legitimate. Under the "typical" formula for blood revenge killings, when a life is being repaid with another life the deaths cancel "each other out...and the way is...open for the restoration of normal peaceful relationships" (Peters 1967: 265). As noted by Karsten (1923: 13) in his study on the Jibaro tribes of Eastern Ecuador, this rule is put in place to limit the destructive potential of blood revenge, as engaging in excessive retaliatory killings "would awaken indignation in the whole tribe." Nevertheless, the "one life for one life" formula does not constitute a universal rule of thumb. The custom of blood revenge amongst Montenegrins has not always abided by the "one-for-one" tenet (Boehm 1984: 216), while Kurdish tribesmen would sometimes kill "not one man but four or five" to restore the balance of honour (Bruinessen 1992: 65).

Regardless of the number of lives deemed as necessary to restore a damaged reputation, the concept of equivalence holds for as long as the killing is regulated according to a collectively accepted rule. To breach the principle of reciprocity offsets the restored balance amongst the two families/clans and, as with the case of the Eskimos living in circumpolar regions, when an avenger kills for a second occasion without justification he becomes "a dangerous public enemy" (Hoebel 2006: 25). This is further confirmed by Miller (1983: 160) in his study on the mechanisms of blood revenge in Mediaeval Iceland and England, where the author specifies that "taking ten lives for one" did not constitute a legitimate act of vengeance, as in the bloodbath there could only be "either war or anarchy."

Blood Revenge and Social Sanctions

For individuals living in honour societies, responding to injuries or insults caused by others fulfils more than "just" a need for deterring deviant behaviour. As Nisbett and Cohen (1996: xvi) specify in their monograph discussing the social order of honour-based cultures, "honour is not merely a self-defence concern: It suffuses all relations." Born and raised in a social environment in which one's reputation is considered the highest social value, every man must be ready to defend his and his family's honour, no matter the cost, because "losing one's face" in front of others would bring about dire consequences. As explained by a tribesman from Kosheh, a village situated in Upper Egypt, "if you kill my brother and I don't kill one of your family, I will be ashamed in the village. Everyone will be talking about me and say he's not a man... It's for the honour of the family" (Lohr 2016).

"Cutting across all other social classifications," writes Peristiany (1965: 10), honour "divides social beings into two fundamental categories, those endowed with honour and those deprived of it." In areas where customary codes regulate social life, "honour establishes status" and a family's wealth and social ranking are secured only insofar as its reputation remains unstained (Pitt-Rivers 1965: 22). For this reason, men consider performing blood revenge killings as their most sacred right and duty. As observed by Tuckerman (1872: 341) during his voyage across the pastoral areas of 19th-century Greece, "a deep-seated injury like wounded honour or a family insult burns like compressed and slow consuming tow," and an insulted man would not find peace "until he has met insult with insult, or blood with blood."

Those who fail to exact blood revenge are ostracised and ridiculed by their communities. While in Corsica, a man who failed to avenge an insult could "no longer appear in public" (Busquet 1919: 357–358), in Kurdish villages "other members of the community harass and censure such a person. He is looked upon as unworthy, cowardly, dishonourable, and even abnormal" (Tezcan 1982: 10). The disdain for cowardice and dishonour prompts avengers not only to seek vengeance but also to feel relief in the cathartic act of retaliation. As described by Djilas (1958: 106) in his memoirs describing life in a rural Montenegrin village, a promise of vengeance made to his dying uncle felt inebriating: "Revenge is an overpowering and consuming fire. It flares up and burns away every other thought and emotion. Only it remains, over and above everything else."

To make things even more severe, the social stigma suffered by an avenger incapable of restoring his honour is cast upon his entire lineage, "for the injury done to one stains the whole house" (Niccolai 1940, cited in Dean 1997: 3). When an avenger fails to take the burden of blood revenge upon himself, all his family members risk being marginalised and treated as "second-class" individuals. Amongst northern Albanian Ghegs, a highlander unable to retaliate risked finding out that "other men had contemptuously come to sleep with his wife, and his daughter could not marry into a 'good' family" (Hasluck 1954: 232). Given the social consequences of living a life in dishonour, avengers are unlikely to abandon their quest for vengeance. As reported by a Chechen describing the social sanctions suffered by individuals breaking the customary law, *adat*, "the disgrace of being a rat would live for generations, being projected not only upon the individual violator of the code of honour, but also upon their clan as a whole" (Souleimanov & Aliyev 2017: 51).

As the social penalties associated with the failure to fulfil one's obligations are intolerably high, in theory, few individuals would risk the consequences of non-compliance with customary laws. Hence, a single act of blood revenge bears the potential for triggering retaliation from the other party, spurring a cycle of tit-for-tat counter-retaliation killings between two rival families—a condition known as "blood feud" (Schumann & Ross 2010).

While feuds might last for generations and, as seldom was the case in ancient Greenland, end up with one side eliminating all the male members of the other (Sonne 1982 31), in most cases the dispute is solved peacefully with the payment of a sum of money as an alternative for the taking of a life (Gluckman 1955). Known as *Diyat* in Islamic jurisprudence (Patton 1901) and *Wergild* in ancient Germanic law (Davies 1969), the practice of accepting blood money to restore one's honour and prevent an escalation of retaliatory killings is rooted in the customary law of many societies. In post-colonial Somalia, the practice of seeking blood money was so widespread that a standard rate of "100 camels for the life of a man and 50 camels for the life of a woman" regulated compensatory transactions (Contini 1971: 78). Similarly, in nowadays' Sudan, the economic benefits of monetary compensations continue persuading many families to prefer blood money over exacting vengeance (Wilson 2014). On other occasions, alternative forms of payment may be accepted. After visiting the Kurdish areas of Northern Iraq, Hay reported that young girls are often gifted to the offended party to end a dispute:

> It is very common for a girl to be given away in marriage in payment of blood-money. Thus if £90 is owing, the price of the blood of one man, the debt might be paid by the delivery of one girl, three cows and a donkey.
>
> (Hay 1921: 73)

The de-escalatory potential of monetary settlements is reinforced by the presence of tribal councils and tribal leaders acting as mediators between families and clans involved in blood-related disputes. As witnessed by a 20th-century ethnographer visiting the tribal areas of Waziristan, every time that an episode of murder or serious injury between tribesmen would occur a group of "men of position and repute" would be selected as arbitrators in charge of defining an appropriate sum of blood-money ("The Blood Feud in Waziristan" 1932: 309). In tribal societies, institutionalised customary systems are extremely widespread. As reported by Chirayath et al. (2005), tribal councils operating across most African countries take care of over 75 percent of the total disputes occurring between and within indigenous communities.

When a dispute is settled by the tribal council, the hostilities must cease at once: "no one can take revenge, so the dispute is over …No one will break the deal because if they do, they might be banished from the tribe, in which case they would die" (Kilcullen 2009: 168). Accordingly, in some societies, the decision to perform a blood revenge murder instead of accepting blood money is to be taken by the tribal leaders on behalf of the entire collective. In their account, based on ethnographic fieldwork, of the tribes inhabiting Central Australia at the end of the 19th century, Spencer and Gillen explain that blood revenge killings could only be accomplished if the tribal elders deemed it as necessary to preserve the collective honour:

> When it is decided who is guilty, a council of the old men of the group to which the dead man belonged is held and, if it be decided that vengeance is to be exacted by means of a Kurdaitcha party, then the man who is to play this part is chosen.
>
> (Spencer & Gillen 1899: 477)

As no rational individual would ever want to see his children and nephews trapped in endless cycles of deadly attacks, most feuds are settled with the payment of blood-money and the return to a condition of peaceful coexistence between the involved parties. As explained by an Afghan Taliban leader, it is the risk of seeing your loved ones killed for crimes that they did not commit that dissuades people from engaging in deviant behaviour:

> If, knowing that your son could pay for a crime committed by some distant cousin with his life, would you not do everything in your power to save them?...Would you not do everything to stop those distant cousins from committing atrocities? Among my tribes, no one will take such a risk, none of our families. They will watch their own, making sure they do not commit any crimes and thereby bring disaster upon their clan.
>
> (Jagielski 2018)

Nonetheless, as an institutionalised mechanism of social control, blood revenge has its own weaknesses and limitations that often arise at times of disorder, political upheaval, or warfare. Amidst the chaos of conflict, tribal leaders may either fall victim to the armed hostilities or lose their status of impartial judges entitled to solve episodes of blood revenge. In insurgent-hit tribal areas of Pakistan, for instance, traditional councils of elders—known as *Jirgas*—are often seen as impartial, corrupt, and illegitimate due to their alleged allegiance to the Pakistani government, which rewards their loyalty with monthly stipends. As reported by Yousaf and FurrikhZad (2020: 1207), the "rent-seeking behaviour" of tribal elders alienated many locals, who no longer entrusted *Jirgas* with the resolution of interpersonal disputes.

For a tribal leader, the act of submission to an external authority often marks the loss of his status as a recognised arbiter amongst his fellow tribesmen, who may feel entitled to disrespect his decisions in matters of law and justice. In the predominantly tribal Governorate of Al-Anbar, in Western Iraq, the rapid recovery of the then Al-Qaeda affiliate, known as Al-Qaeda in Iraq (AQI), in mid-2006 cowed many tribal leaders into submission, with severe repercussions for their social status. As explained by Cigar, the inability to punish AQI elements for their disregard for tribal customs threatened to erode the sheiks' ability to enforce their decisions:

> If a shaykh is unable to defend his tribe's honor, he not only loses face but this can also call into question a shaykh's ability and willingness

to protect fellow tribesmen— all key aspects of a shaykh's standing and legitimacy.

(Cigar 2011: 19)

When the status of tribal leaders and village elders is compromised, some members of the community may disregard traditional conflict resolution mechanisms in favour of violent redress. A sheikh from the Al-Jawf Governorate, in Northern Yemen, explained that years of violence and conflict have eroded the stance of tribal leaders in the area, so much so that young people often feel that "they are their own sheikh" entitled to act irrespectively of their leaders' decisions (Al-Dawsari 2012: 10).

The ability of traditional authority figures to mediate disputes and de-escalate blood feuds can be further damaged when their actions are seen as cowardly, weak, or otherwise disdainful, especially in matters of tribal honour and sociocultural customs. During the First Russian-Chechen War of 1994–1996, countless Chechen village elders lost the respect of their communities after coming to terms with the Russian invading force. As Cheterian explained in his monograph on the North Caucasian insurgency, the village elders' loss of social status contributed to inflating instances of blood revenge killings in the conflict's aftermath:

> The war of 1994–1996 destroyed the social tissue and the last institution respected in Chechen society, that of the clan elders. Advancing Russian troops often negotiated with the village elders to convince the Chechen resistance fighters to abandon their positions... After the fighters retook these regions in the summer of 1996, they no longer responded to the institution of the elders, because in their eyes those elders who had negotiated with the Russian occupants had lost legitimacy and respect ... This left [the] Chechen society without the traditional mediator, the judge and the moral reference which since old times had been the institution to settle daily conflicts. The result was a proliferation of violence.

(Cheterian 2008: 343)

The erosion of the village elders' authority during the First Russian-Chechen War was further aggravated during the Second Russian-Chechen War of 1999–2009. Although nationalist-inspired rebel groups typically felt duty-bound to respect the authority of tribal elders, many jihadi militants despised customary laws in favour of Islamic principles. The jihadists' refusal to submit to the village elders' authority contributed to accelerating their loss of status, with the consequence that many individuals eventually decided to take up arms instead of resorting to traditional conflict resolution mechanisms (Souleimanov & Siroky 2016: 703).

At times of war and political instability, the shortcomings of traditional conflict resolution mechanisms may remove the structural conditions inhibiting the escalatory potential of blood revenge, with the consequence that avengers are often left with no other choice but to engage in retaliatory violence to restore their families' honour. This inherent weakness, in turn, is one of the chief causes of the decline of blood revenge in modern societies, where the recourse to retributive violence progressively comes to be seen as socially unacceptable. Armed with this conceptualisation of blood revenge, Chapter 3 traces the causal mechanisms leading to the erosion and resurgence of this age-old custom.

References

"The Blood Feud in Waziristan," *Journal of the Royal Central Asian Society* 19(2), 1932: 304–310. DOI: 10.1080/03068373208725207

Aase, H. Tor. "The Grammar of Honour and Revenge," *Journal of Law and Social Research* 20(10), 2013: 1–20. https://tidsskrift.dk/nnjlsr/article/view/111 092/160170

Al-Dawsari, Nadwa. "Tribal Governance and Stability in Yemen," *Carnegie Endowment for International Peace, Middle East,* April 2012. Available at: https://carnegieendowment.org/files/yemen_tribal_governance.pdf

Barclay, Harold. *People without Government: An Anthropology of Anarchy* (London: Kahn & Averill, 1990). ISBN 1-871082-16-1.

Barnes, D. Collin; Brown, P. Ryan & Osterman, L. Lindsey. "Don't Tread on Me: Masculine Honor Ideology in the US and Militant Responses to Terrorism," *Personality and Social Psychology Bulletin* 38(8), 2012: 1018–1029. DOI: 10.1177/0146167212443383

Benson, L. Bruce. "Legal Evolution in Primitive Societies," *Journal of Institutional and Theoretical Economics* 144(5), 1988: 772–788. www.jstor.org/stable/40751135

Boehm, Christopher. *Blood Revenge: The Enactment and Management of Conflict in Montenegro and Other Tribal Societies* (Philadelphia: University of Pennsylvania Press, 1984). ISBN: 081221241X.

Boyle, J. Michael. "Revenge and Reprisal Violence in Kosovo," *Conflict, Security & Development* 10(2), 2010: 189–216. DOI: 10.1080/14678801003665968

Bruinessen, Martin. *Agha, Shaikh and State: The Social and Political Structures of Kurdistan* (London: Zeb Books Ltd, 1992). ISBN-10: 185649019X.

Burckhardt, L. John. *Notes on the Bedouins and Wahabys: Collected During His Travels in the East* (London: A. J. Valpy, 1831).

Busquet, Jacques. *Le Droit De La Vendetta et Les 'Paci' Corses* (Paris: A. Pedone, 1919). ISBN-10: 2735502961.

Chagnon, Napoleon. "Life Histories, Blood Revenge, and Warfare in a Tribal Population," *Science* 239 (4843), 1988: 985–992. www.jstor.org/stable/1700080

Cheterian, Vicken. *War and Peace in the Caucasus: Russia's Troubled Frontier* (London: Hurst & Co, 2008). ISBN: 9781850659877.

Chirayath, Leila; Sage, Caroline & Woolcock, Michael. "Customary Law and Policy Reform: Engaging with the Plurality of Justice Systems," Conference Paper, *World Development Report 2006: Equity and Development*, 2005. http://hdl.handle.net/10986/9075

Cigar, Norman. *Al-Qaida, the Tribes, and the Government: Lessons and Prospects for Iraq's Unstable Triangle* (Quantico: Marine Corps University Press, 2011). ISBN: 1512307092.

Cohen-Mor, Dalya. *Fathers and Sons in the Arab Middle East* (New York: Palgrave Macmillan, 2013). ISBN-10: 1349462942.

Contini, Paolo. "The Evolution of Blood-Money for Homicide in Somalia," *Journal of African Law* 15(1), 1971: 77–84. www.jstor.com/stable/744600

Czaplicka, A. M. *Aboriginal Siberia: A Study in Social Anthropology* (Oxford: Clarendon Press, 1914). ISBN-10: 0353468339.

Davies, R. "The Survival of the Bloodfeud in Mediaeval Wales," *History* 54, 1969: 338–357. https://doi.org/10.1111/j.1468-229X.1969.tb02328.x

Dean, Trevor. "Marriage and Mutilation: Vendetta in Late Mediaeval Italy," *Past & Present* 157, 1997: 3–36. www.jstor.org/stable/651079

Djilas, Milovan. *Land Without Justice* (New York: Harcourt, Brace and Company, 1958). ISBN-10: 0156481170.

Evans-Pritchard, E. E. *The Nuer: A Description of the Modes of Livelihood and Political Institutions of a Nilotic People* (Oxford: The Clarendon Press, 1940). ISBN-10: 0195003225.

Frijda, H. Nico & Mesquita, Batja. "Beliefs through Emotions" in *Emotions and Beliefs*, edited by Frijda, H. Nico; Manstead, S. R. Antony & Bem, Sacha (Cambridge: Cambridge University Press, 2000), 45–77. ISBN: 9780511659904.

Gluckman, Max. "The Peace in the Feud," *Past & Present* 8, 1955: 1–14. www.jstor.org/stable/649774

Halsall, Guy. "Reflections on Early Medieval Violence: The Example of the 'Blood Feud'," *Memoria y Civilización* 2, 1999: 7–29. DOI:10.15581/001.2.33918

Hasluck, Margaret. *The Unwritten Law in Albania* (Cambridge: Cambridge University Press, 1954). ISBN: 1107586933.

Hay, R. William. *Two Years in Kurdistan: Experiences of a Political Officer, 1918–1920* (London: Sidgwick & Jackson, 1921).

Hinton, L. Alexander. "A Head for an Eye: Revenge in the Cambodian Genocide," *American Ethnologist* 25(3), 1998: 352–377. www.jstor.org/stable/645789

Hobfoll, E. Stevan. *Tribalism. The Evolutionary Origins of Fear Politics* (New York: Palgrave Macmillan, 2018). ISBN-10: 3319784048.

Hoebel, E. Adamson. *The Law of Primitive Man: A Study in Comparative Legal Dynamics* (Cambridge: Harvard University Press, 2006). ISBN: 9780674038707.

Jagielski, Wojciech. "Blood for Blood," *PrzeKrój*, September 3, 2018. Available at: https://przekroj.pl/en/society/blood-for-blood-wojciech-jagielski

Kaminsky, Howard. "The Noble Feud in the Later Middle Ages," *Past & Present* 177, 2002: 55–83. www.jstor.com/stable/3600878

Karsten, Rafel. *Blood Revenge, War, and Victory Feasts among the Jibaro Indians of Eastern Ecuador* (Washington: Government Printing Office, 1923).

Kilcullen, David. *The Accidental Guerrilla: Fighting Small Wars in the Midst of a Big One* (New York: Oxford University Press, 2009). ISBN-10: 9780199754090.

Kuschel, Rolf. "Killing Begets Killing: Homicides and Blood Feuds on a Polynesian Outlier," *Bijdragen tot de Taal-, Land- en Volkenkunde* 149(4), 1993: 690–717. www.jstor.org/stable/27864498

Lee, E. Wayne. "Peace Chiefs and Blood Revenge: Patterns of Restraint in Native American Warfare, 1500–1800," *The Journal of Military History* 71(3), 701–741. https://doi.org/10.1353/jmh.2007.0216

Lohr, Sabina. "The Tradition of Family Revenge Killings in Upper Egypt," *Connect the Cultures*, September 19, 2016. Available at: www.connecttheculturres.com/revenge-killings-upper-egypt/

MacCormack, Geoffrey. "Revenge and Compensation in Early Law," *The American Journal of Comparative Law* 21(1), 1973: 69–85. www.jstor.org/stable/839418

Matikainen, Olli. *Recovering Blood: Violence and Community in the Age of Transition, the Case of Eastern Finland from the Middle Ages until 1700* (Helsinki: Finnish Literature Society (SKS), 2002). ISBN: 954-746-268-9.

McCabe, David. *How to Kill Things with Words: Ananias and Sapphira under the Prophetic Speech-Act of Divine Judgement* (London: A Continuum Imprint, 2011). ISBN: 9780567525437.

Meier, D. Larissa. "The Strategic Use of Emotions in Recruitment Strategies of Armed Groups: The Case of the Liberation Tigers of Tamil Eelam," *Studies in Conflict & Terrorism* 44(12), 2019: 1–19. DOI:10.1080/1057610X.2019.1634343

Miller, William. "Choosing the Avenger: Some Aspects of the Bloodfeud in Medieval Iceland and England," *Law and History Review* 1(2), 1983: 159–204. https://doi.org/10.2307/743849

Mills, D. "Kataki-Uchi: The Practice of Blood-Revenge in Pre-Modern Japan," *Modern Asian Studies* 10(4), 1976: 525–542. https://doi.org/10.1017/S0026749X00014943

Nisbett, E. Richard & Cohen, Dov. *Culture of Honor: The Psychology of Violence in the South* (Boulder: Westview, 1996). ISBN: 978-0813319933.

Patton, M. Walter. "Blood-Revenge in Arabia and Israel," *The American Journal of Theology* 5(4), 1901: 703–731. www.jstor.org/stable/3152697

Peristiany, G. J. "Introduction" in *Honour and Shame*, edited by Peristiany, G. J. (London: Weidenfeld & Nicolson, 1965), 9–18.

Perrin, Chris. "Of Grey Geese and Burning Lawyers: The Structures of the Feud System in Viking Age Iceland," *The Graduate History Review* 5(1),

2016: 139–168. Available at: https://journals.uvic.ca/index.php/ghr/article/view/13281

Peters, L. E. "Some Structural Aspects of the Feud among the Camel-Herding Bedouin of Cyrenaica," *Africa: Journal of the International African Institute* 37(3), 1967: 261–282. https://doi.org/10.2307/1158150

Pitt-Rivers, Julian. 'Honour and Social Status' in *Honour and Shame*, edited by Peristiany, G. J. (London: Weidenfeld & Nicolson, 1965), 19–78.

Reed, J. Brian & Segal, R. David. "Capture of Saddam Hussein: Social Network Analysis and Counterinsurgency Operations" in *The Routledge Handbook of War and Society: Iraq and Afghanistan*, edited by Carlton-Ford, Steven & Ender, Morten G. (London: Routledge, 2011), 68–77. ISBN: 9780415567329.

Renteln, D. Alison. "A Cross-Cultural Approach to Validating International Human Rights: The Case of Retribution Tied to Proportionality" in *Human Rights: Theory and Measurement*, edited by Cingranelli, L. David (London: The Macmillan Press, 1988), 7–40. ISBN: 978-1-349-10122-1.

Robinson, E. A. "Women and Blood Revenge," *Sudan Notes and Records* 4(2), 1921: 107–108. www.jstor.org/stable/41715707

Rosenthal, T. Joel. "Marriage and the Blood Feud in 'Heroic Europe'," *The British Journal of Sociology* 17(2), June 1966: 133–144. www.jstor.org/stable/589052

Rukaj, Marjola. "Albania: If the Kanun Degenerates," *Osservatorio Balcani e Caucaso*, July 31, 2012. Available at: www.balcanicaucaso.org/eng/Areas/Albania/Albania-if-the-Kanun-degenerates-120698

Schumann, Karina & Ross, Michael. "The Benefits, Costs, and Paradox of Revenge," *Social and Personality Psychology Compass* 4(12), 2010: 1193–1205. https://doi.org/10.1111/j.1751-9004.2010.00322.x

Sonne, Birgitte. "The Ideology and Practice of Blood Feuds in East and West Greenland," *Études/Inuit/Studies* 6(2), 1982: 21–50. www.jstor.org/stable/42869352

Souleimanov, A. Emil & Aliyev, Huseyn. "Blood Revenge and Violent Mobilization: Evidence from the Chechen Wars," *International Security* 40(2), 2015: 158–180. DOI: 10.1162/ISEC_a_00219

Souleimanov, A. Emil & Aliyev, Huseyn. *How Socio-Cultural Codes Shaped Violent Mobilisation and Pro-insurgent Support in the Chechen Wars* (Basingstoke: Palgrave Macmillian, 2017). ISBN: 9783319529165.

Souleimanov, A. Emil & Siroky, S. David. "Random or Retributive?: Indiscriminate Violence in the Chechen Wars," *World Politics* 68(4), 2016: 677–712. DOI: 10.1017/S0043887116000101

Spencer, Baldwin & Gillen, F.J. *The Native Tribes of Central Australia* (London: Macmillan & Co., 1899).

Tamut, Rebecca. "Blood Feud in the Eastern Himalaya: An Account of a Forgotten Massacre of Police Personnel in Nefa, India," *Anthropos* 114, 2019: 97–105. https://doi.org/10.5771/0257-9774-2019-1-97

Tezcan, Mahmut. "The Tradition of Blood Feuds in Turkey." *Turkish Studies Association Bulletin* 6(1), 1982: 7–13. www.jstor.org/stable/43385106

Thrasher, John & Handfield, Toby. "Honor and Violence: An Account of Feuds, Duels, and Honor Killings," *Human Nature* 29, 2018: 371–389. DOI: 10.1007/s12110-018-9324-4

Tsantiropoulos, Aris. "Collective Memory and Blood Feud; The Case of Mountainous Crete." *Crimes and Misdemeanours* 2(1), 2008: 60–80. http://hdl.handle.net/10026.1/8832

Tuckerman, K. Charles. *The Greeks of To-Day* (New York: G. P. Putnam & Sons, 1872).

Vaporis, N. Constantine. "Samurai, Masculinity and Violence in Japan" in *The Cambridge History of Violence*, Volume III, edited by Antony, Robert; Carroll, Stuart & Pennock, D. Caroline (Cambridge: Cambridge University Press, 2020), 236–254. ISBN: 9781316340592.

Waldmann, Peter. "Revenge Without Rules: On the Renaissance of an Archaic Motif of Violence," *Studies in Conflict and Terrorism* 24(6), 2001: 435–450. https://doi.org/10.1080/105761001753210470

Wallace-Hadrill, J. Michael. "The Bloodfeud of the Franks," *Bulletin of the John Rylands Library* 41(2), 1959: 459–487. DOI: 10.7227/bjrl.41.2.10.

Wilson, H. Jacqueline. "Blood Money in Sudan and Beyond: Restorative Justice or Face-Saving Measure?" PhD Thesis, Georgetown University, 2014. http://hdl.handle.net/10822/709806

Wood, C. John. "Conceptualizing Cultures of Violence and Cultural Change" in *Cultures of Violence*, edited by Carroll, Stuart (Houndmills: Palgrave Macmillan, 2006), 79–98. ISBN: 9780230591820.

Yousaf, Farooq & FurrikhZad, Syed. "Pashtun Jirga and Prospects of Peace and Conflict Resolution in Pakistan's 'Tribal' Frontier," *Third World Quarterly* 41(7), 2020: 1200–1217. DOI: 10.1080/01436597.2020.1760088

3 The Erosion of Blood Revenge in Modern Society

Having regulated the inter-communal life of many societies before its erosion, blood revenge constitutes a resilient custom which, as Wormald (1980: 83) argues, can hardly be suppressed by "mounting a full frontal attack on it." While case study research implicitly agrees with Wormald's consideration, diverging interpretations of this custom greatly influence the general perception of the mechanisms engendering its decline. Derived from a lack of in-depth, comparative research conducted on the contextual factors accompanying the erosion of blood revenge, these diverging conceptions threaten to compartmentalise the collective understanding of this complex phenomenon.

At one end of the spectrum, scholars have induced from single case study research that the process of state centralisation constitutes the principal factor prompting the demise of blood revenge. By far constituting the dominant viewpoint, this perspective is embodied in studies carried out on state-building efforts that occurred in early societies. According to Lendon's (2000: 12) account of state formation dynamics in ancient Greece, "the old culture of self-help had yielded to the institutions of the nascent *polis*; blood revenge yielded to the courts of the city." Conversely, other scholars have implicitly suggested that, in specific cases, the revolutionary changes brought about by the birth of modern society engendered the disappearance of blood revenge. "The truth," writes Bedford (1939: 223) in his article discussing the decline of honour culture in 19th-century England, is that the imperative of defending one's honour by recurring to violence "was one of the institutions which were killed by the Industrial Revolution and the social changes which accompanied it."

From these two contrasting yet reconcilable views, we propose a critical examination of the principal causes for the decline of blood revenge, extracting from anthropological and sociological literature the evidence to illustrate how these mechanisms apply to the empirical world. This extensive review shows that, for blood revenge to erode and wither

DOI: 10.4324/9781003387527-3

away, the processes of state centralisation and societal rejection must occur in sequence. Each mechanism encompasses two distinctive sub-mechanisms—all of which mark a specific stage in the decline of blood revenge. It is the cumulative concatenation of these mechanisms, rather than their isolated occurrence, that erodes the structural and societal underpinnings of blood revenge, which progressively transitions from a highly institutionalised sociocultural custom to a loosely regulated instrument of self-help justice, before being rejected as a socially acceptable practice. As this chapter shows, the failure of any of these sub-mechanisms is likely to breathe new life into blood revenge, as further confirmation of their equally important relevance for the success of the overall process. Recognising their concatenating effect allows for a more comprehensive appreciation of the causes leading to the erosion of blood revenge.

In conceptualising the mechanisms of state centralisation and societal rejection of blood revenge as mutually reinforcing and complementary, this chapter argues that blood revenge is likely to wither away only when both factors work in sequence over a prolonged time period. When the erosion of blood revenge does not lead to the complete dissolution of the culture of honour, people may still consider retaliation as a viable and socially sanctioned response to perceived wrongs or insults. This condition, defined in this book as a "culture of retaliation," endures at a subterranean level and can resurface at times of war with important implications for the conduct of irregular warfare.

State Centralisation

Rooted in the sociological thought of Max Weber (1946 [1921]: 1), the "state centralisation" narrative considers the disappearance of blood revenge as contingent upon the emergence of the state, "a human community that successfully claims the monopoly of the legitimate use of physical force within a given territory." Prompted by the gradual strengthening of a central political entity, the transition from a condition of blood feud to one of institutionalised justice is considered in Weberian terms as a transition to "a form of permanent public peace, with the compulsory submission of all disputes to the arbitration of the judge, who transforms blood vengeance into rationally ordered punishment" (Weber 1978 [1922]: 908).

This interpretation, which draws upon traditional 19th-century concepts from the field of legal anthropology, finds widespread support in the literature on customary practices. In their book on the historical evolution of legal systems in Early Mediaeval England, Pollock and Maitland (2009 [1898]: 31) argue that the progressive centralisation of power structures was the root cause for the disappearance of the blood feud: "Step-by-step, as the power of the State waxes, the self-centred and self-helping of the kindred wanes. Private feud is controlled, regulated, put … into legal harness." Similarly, in his account of blood revenge practices in pre-modern Japan, Mills (1976: 528) explains how the act of avenging a fallen kinsman was progressively incorporated into the legal system of the nascent Japanese state, which turned it into a highly regulated legal procedure before "abruptly" criminalising it during the 19th century.

Within this theoretical paradigm, scholars identify two sub-mechanisms: the centralisation of judicial power by a political entity on one side, and the penalisation of the illegal use of lethal force on the other. We closely examine these two interlinked factors, illustrating how the process of state centralisation prompts the gradual erosion of violent customary practices.

Judicial Centralisation

To claim its monopoly over the legitimate use of force, an authority must discourage its subjects from seeking private redress by offering a viable alternative for the settlement of conflicts. Under the king's peace, blood revenge gradually loses momentum as the central authority's courts assert their prerogative over the resolution of criminal law matters. Yet, blood revenge does not disappear "with marvellous suddenness" as soon as the state deploys a specialised staff of judicial enforcers. Instead, the process can require decades, if not centuries to come to fruition (Wormald 1980: 95).

In ancient China, the custom of blood revenge was enshrined in traditional Confucian culture, which was centred upon the moral imperative of preserving family honour and social status. As shown by a passage from the *LiJi*, an early collection of Chinese customary codes, avengers were expected to diligently carry out blood revenge to restore their families' honour:

> A son must not live under the same sky with the murderer of his father; he must seek to fight with him under either he or his enemy should be killed. If his brother has been murdered, one should always carry arms along with him; so that in case he met the enemy, he might not lose the opportunity of executing vengeance upon him.
>
> (Wu 1921: 512)

As the imperial dynasties got stronger and more capable of administering law and order, however, laws were put in place to contain blood feuds and prevent the population from invoking customary codes as a legitimate basis for carrying out homicides with impunity. As showed by Dalby (1981: 307) in his study of the Qing empire's (1644–1912) approach to the administering of justice, the Manchu-led imperial authorities underwent "strenuous efforts ... to reduce revenge, so far as possible, to a single, legally apprehensible incident arising from and affecting relationships between individuals [rather than entire (sub)ethnic or kinship groups]."

The decline in revenge-related crimes in the 16th- and 17th-century Scotland reiterates the evolutionary trends identified in the previous case. To suppress such a deep-rooted custom, the Scottish crown waged a long war against it, a struggle made possible by the joint effort of local lords, privy councils, and professional lawyers (Wormald 1980). As expounded by Brown, by the early 17th century, the combined action of royal decrees and local initiatives reduced and ultimately inhibited the population's recourse to self-help justice:

> After 1603 the amount of feuding had dropped to some forty to fifty feuds a year from the high point of sixty to seventy during the 1590's ... the fall was fairly regular, dropping to under ten in 1625. Of all the feuds in Scotland over the entire period over 75 percent of them were at one point or another handled by the government.
>
> (Brown 1983: 579)

In Corsica, the French government followed a similar approach to uproot blood revenge. In enforcing the government's rule over the island, the French monarchy established a dense network of state-controlled justice courts. As remarked by Raggio (1990: 943) in his analysis of France's strategy in Corsica, "the island abounded with justice courts and peace officers: throughout the 19th century, the size of the judicial personnel in Corsica was three times larger than in any other French department."

Pressured by the ubiquitous presence of the government's judicial apparatus, the population progressively relinquished self-help justice and instances of blood revenge started becoming a rarity. As reported by Wilson (2002: 265), during the second half of the 19th century, most Corsicans utilised "their pens instead of their daggers and conduct[ed] their vendettas with pieces of paper." These claims are consistent with a study by Gould (2000: 689) who, after examining a large volume of court records from the 19th-century Corsica, finds that vendetta-motivated homicides remained below a 15 percent rate, suggesting that "most of the time the island's inhabitants left the pursuit of justice to the courts."

At times, this process is facilitated by the gradual incorporation of traditional conflict resolution mechanisms within the state's own judicial system. In many societies where blood revenge endures, the payment of blood money by the offender not only exempts the injured party from exacting revenge but also makes it dishonourable, for the latter, to pursue vengeance if the former complies with the peaceful settlement of the dispute. In Viking-Age Iceland, individuals who decided against respecting a peaceful settlement were dishonoured by their peers and called *griðniðingr* (settlement breakers), a strong derogatory term reserved for cowards and traitors. This is typified in a section of a Nordic Saga reported by Byock (2003: 240), in which an individual called out for not having avenged his father justifies his actions by referring to a previous peaceful settlement: "I was a child when he was killed, and my kinsmen took up the case. They arranged a settlement on my behalf, and among us, it does not sit well to be called by the name of *griðniðingr.*"

Today, the incorporation of blood money practices within the state's legal system can be observed across many countries where traditional customary codes are still in place. In the islands of Papua New Guinea, local courts "openly encourage" the principle of blood money, so much so that judges routinely order the payment of a sum of money to the injured party to mitigate the recurrence of payback killings and deter people from taking the law "into their own hands" (Gordon 1981: 97). Similarly, the payment of blood money (*diya*) finds application in the legal systems of many Middle Eastern countries, including Qatar, Iran, and the United Arab Emirates, where sums of blood money due to the offended party are determined based on the severity of the crime and regulated according to inflation and market prices (Hassanein 2018; Pascoe 2016; Center for Human Rights in Iran 2017). Although the state's acceptance of blood money as a legitimate form of compensation for a crime raises criticisms on moral grounds, its adoption likely contributes to mitigating the incidence of inter-communal violence and lowers the number of people killed in blood revenge disputes (Akyol 2020).

Penalisation of Blood Revenge

If incentivising people to peacefully solve their feuds in justice courts can be conceived as the "persuasive" approach to the uprooting of traditional customs, the penalisation of recidivist behaviours constitutes the opposite, darker face of top-down suppressive efforts. Described by Frost and d'Anglure (2015: 232) as a "war on murder," the state's compelling desire to monopolise the use of force can often result in a radical crackdown on individuals willing to defy the government's authority.

The extirpation of customary laws carried out by Soviet officers in Georgia during the Stalinist era exemplifies this "iron fist" strategy.

Considered as a "harmful threat" to Moscow's authority, the local tradition of self-help justice was severely criminalised under Soviet law, with state legislators "punishing specific offences harder when they (were) committed in the name of tradition" (Janiashvili 2016: 91). A particularly harsh treatment was reserved to individuals involved in blood feuds. As remarked by Jalabadze and Janiashvili (2016), local justice enforcers followed the Soviet criminal code when dealing with individuals guilty of having performed an act of blood-taking, typically sentencing the prisoner to death by firing squad. Today, rare cases of blood feuds still take place amongst the Svans, an ethnic group traditionally living across the mountainous regions of Svaneti and Khevsureti (Jalabadze 2012). As explained by a local tribal leader, the collapse of the Soviet regime gave new impetus to blood feuds, calling for the restoration of customary conflict resolution mechanisms to prevent the return of blood feuds (Larmer 2014).

A similar pattern characterises the gradual erosion of blood revenge in modern-day Azerbaijan. During the Soviet era, most Azerbaijanis were compelled to abandon the "old ways" of settling interpersonal disputes under the threat of severe punishment. Yet, the fall of the Soviet regime breathed new life into the largely eroded custom. During an interview with a local newspaper, an Azerbaijani villager told how his grandmother was stabbed to death in 1998 by a 15-year-old boy, who wished to exact vengeance for a murder which took place decades earlier:

> when we found out who the murderer was, everything became clear to everyone. Those [the young boy's relatives] were blood enemies of our family … when my grandfather was young, he had killed a child from that family who was the 15-year-old boy's uncle.
>
> (Meydan TV 2019)

Episodes of blood revenge continue to occur from time to time in the country, mostly carried out by individuals who lost trust in the Azerbaijani judicial system and decided to revert to customary codes out of the desire to "get even" with the perceived culprit (Medzhid 2019).

Often deemed as necessary to devitalise a powerful mechanism of anti-incumbent mobilisation, the suppression of blood revenge was particularly assertive in Albania during the Communist dictatorship of Enver Hoxha (1946–1985). To crush the opposition to his rule and enforce Tirana's supremacy over the population, Hoxha waged a campaign of systematic suppression of customary codes and clan-based power structures (Plaku et al. 2019). Under the new regime, any act of blood revenge—especially if performed against state officials—was severely criminalised under the official criminal code and punished accordingly with either deportation or death by execution (Celik & Shkreli 2010: 893). According to statistics provided by the Albanian Ministry of Justice, the government's efforts aimed at enforcing law and order brought the custom of blood revenge towards near eradication: "[In the years] 1951–1955 there is a decrease of blood feud murders of 13.5% and, from 1956 to 1982, there is no [recorded] evidence of any blood feud murder" (Tepshi 2015: 203).

Nevertheless, the fall of the Communist regime in 1991 removed the structural conditions that deterred people from exacting blood revenge, thus giving rise to "a mushrooming of extra-judicial killings caused by the settling of old scores" (Lawson & Douglas 2000: 138). As confirmed by a report published by the Belgian Office of the Commissioner General for Refugees and Stateless Persons, the vacuum caused by the abrupt collapse of the Albanian law enforcement system gave new life to the customary practice of blood revenge, which grew both in popularity and diffusion: "the issue came back to the surface in the 1990s and it revived because of the vacuum of state power" (Cedoca 2017: 10). Although no precise statistics are available on the victims of Albanian blood feuds, there is little doubt that hundreds have been killed in retaliatory attacks and that many others live under the constant threat of being killed by their blood enemies (Government of Canada 2008; Hosken & Kasapi 2017).

Societal Rejection

To uproot blood revenge, top-down suppressive endeavours do not suffice; society must come to reject as inappropriate the recourse to self-help justice on the one hand, and violence directed against the transgressor's relatives on the other. In Lebanon, cycles of blood revenge continue to spiral out of control despite the presence of capable law enforcement agencies and competent justice courts. Following a series of blood revenge murders that unfolded across the Beqaa Governorate in 2020, a Lebanese government official explained that customary codes centred on concepts of honour and revenge remain the cornerstone of the local sociocultural milieu: "Even if official authorities do their job, it's not enough. They [the clans] say that they can only clean their dignity with blood" (Chaoul 2020).

Triggered by the sociocultural changes that accompanied the birth of modern society, the process of societal rejection of kinship-centred vengeance, hence the custom of blood revenge itself, occurs in two phases. The erosion of kinship ties and the downfall of the culture of honour constitute the first part of this process. According to Durkheim, the birth of modern society inhibited those "wild passions" that culminate in blood feud, as the externalities of our inner impulses have become "increasingly cold, reflective, rational" (Grutzpalk 2002: 128; Durkheim 1992 [1957]: 119). With the culture of honour disaggregating under the pressure exercised by a new "enlightened" society, individuals gradually ceased considering "absurd acts of violence" as legitimate means for seeking satisfaction (Durkheim 1984 [1893]: 48).

The decline of the culture of honour is reinforced by the collective anaesthetisation of "irrational" pulses compelling individuals to seek vengeance, a phenomenon that Norbert Elias (2013) defined as a "civilising process." According to this theory, societies living under a centralised authority "exert a constant, even pressure [on individuals] to inhibit affective outbursts," incentivising people to control and rationalise their emotions (Ibid.: 373). In other words, Elias sustains that, in modern societies, individuals are socialised into a collective system that, while stigmatising the use of retributive violence as socially unacceptable, rewards one's ability to repress his primordial impulses: "this self-restraint is ingrained so deeply from an early age that, like a kind of relay-station of social standards, an automatic self-supervision of their drives ... develops" (Ibid.: 374). Building upon Durkheim and Elias's sociological theories, we illustrate how the societal rejection of blood revenge occurs within real-life contexts.

Downfall of the Culture of Honour

In societies with strong concepts of honour and revenge, extended kinship and clan ties constitute the very foundation of social organisation and collective identity. As found by Nuttall (2000: 42) during his ethnographic fieldwork amongst Greenlandic Inuit, the concept of kinship ties extends far beyond the nuclear family, encompassing a wide array of individuals not necessarily linked by close blood relations: "[for Inuit inhabiting the village of Kangersuatsiaq,] kinship is multifaceted, embracing genealogy, consanguinity, affinity, friendship, name-sharing, birthday partners, age-sets, the living and the dead." When injuries or insults suffered by an individual are cast upon his entire extended kinship group, blood revenge is unlikely to subside due to the readiness of each member to safeguard the group's collective honour.

The resilience of blood revenge wanes when powerful changes in the structural conditions of society engender a weakening of kinship ties. Processes of "individualisation, secularisation and globalisation" can markedly transform kinship ties, which come to be perceived no longer as immutable but rather "adjusted, created, and maintained" by individuals according to their own perception of who is kin, and who is not (Lorentzen & Hustinx 2007: 104; Gazso & McDaniel 2015: 376). Eroded by the processes of modernisation and urbanisation, family structures based on extended kinship ties start giving way to atomised families, where membership is granted only to a close group of individuals sharing blood relations amongst each other. This is the case of Algeria, where the nuclear family is "fast becoming the most prevalent family structure" (Deeb 1994: 100), and Oman, where individuals living in urban settings showcase "significantly weaker tribal ties" in comparison to their fellow tribesmen situated in rural areas (Barber 2007: 1).

The progressive weakening of kinship ties inhibits the incidence of blood revenge. As distant relatives are no longer deemed as affiliated with the direct culprit, the pool of individuals eligible for a blood revenge killing shrinks considerably to only encompass the closest members of the nuclear family. Drawing upon evidence collected during an ethnographic field trip across the villages of Shara Valley, Northern Albania, Mustafa and Young (2008: 92) found that the nuclear family has now supplanted clan-based structures as "the kinship unit relevant to the blood feud," further adding that "it is the nuclear family that often carries the burden of revenge and … manages their own feud relations." Similarly, in their study on the role of blood revenge in the North Caucasian Republic of Dagestan, Ratelle and Souleimanov (2017: 575) observed that the disaggregation of local clan structures incentivised the population to consider the practice of targeting an individual's relatives as "socially unacceptable." Weakened by the declining importance of kinship ties, blood revenge loses its moral status in post-honour cultures which, according to Durkheim (1984 [1893]: 48), come to consider as backward any "blind" display of violent retributive behaviour.

The societal rejection of kinship-centred violent reciprocity in contemporary Eritrea exemplifies the trend towards a blood revenge-free society. Initiated by the criminalisation of feuds under the Italian colonial occupation (1882–1941) and enabled by the presence of effective reconciliatory mechanisms at the local level, the decline in blood revenge attacks signals an increasing rejection of vengeance as a socially acceptable means for settling interpersonal disputes (Giorgi 2010). Although the lack of a centralised judicial system prevents the Eritrean society from abandoning customary laws, instances of individuals performing acts of blood revenge have become sporadic. As specified by Favali and Paterman (2003: 103) in their analysis of Eritrea's legal system, "cases of murder are usually settled through the payment of blood money," and instances of people refusing to do so are uncommon due to the collective pressure exercised on both parts to come to a peaceful agreement. In fact, the increasing acceptability of blood money could be seen as a sign of gradual departure from the custom of blood revenge.

While, in Eritrea, the erosion of honour values is still far from being mature, the fast-paced modernisation processes experienced by Sardinia's pastoral communities minimised the recurrence of blood feuds on the island. Once an archetype of a society reliant on customary laws, nowadays Sardinia appears radically different from its 20th-century counterpart. According to a report sponsored by the University of Sassari on the criminal activities registered in Sardinia, instances of blood revenge have become "absolutely residual," as the "socio-cultural and economic context giving rise to this custom … fragmented and rapidly dissolved under the pressure exercised by the modernisation processes that interested the island" (Mazzette et al. 2011: 28).

The slow but uninterrupted decline of the honour culture in Greece shows similarities with the Sardinian case. Pressured by their leaders to abandon customs considered as "non-Western" and therefore uncivilised throughout the 19th and 20th centuries, the Greek pastoral communities progressively drifted apart from their traditional ways of life, preserving most of their old customs in "gesture, dress, and linguistic behaviour" and only rarely acting in accordance with the old ways (Gallant 2002; Herzfeld 1988: 47). As noted by Gallant (2000: 382) in his analysis of the current state of the honour culture in Greece, "men duelled over honour with words, not with stilettos … Losing one's face increasingly became a figure of speech rather than a fact of life."

Rise of the Rational Self-controller

With the sociocultural norms regulating life in societies centred on notions of honour deteriorating under the pressure exercised by the rise of the modern nation state, individuals are increasingly compelled to control their impulses to adjust to the new social environment. Stigmatised as a form of deviancy by the new "civilised" community, in many societies, blood revenge started being considered as a form of irrational violence that "never solves anything" (Bowman 2009: 32). As noted by Miller (1999: 72), in non-honour societies, revenge "becomes either smallminded or vulgarly laud and adolescent … a source of embarrassment to the refined and civilised that needed to be glossed over and carried out in disguise, if carried out at all."

This is consistent with the findings from recent research on the decline of the concepts of honour and violence in many contemporary Western countries. In his authoritative book on the rise and fall of the honour culture, psychologist James Bowman explains that the collective disapproval of violent practices pushed the cultural drive of responding to violence with violence at the margins of society:

> Obviously, if all violence is deplorable and shameful (even if not always or necessarily wrong), cultural honour must wither away, and that is precisely what we have seen in the West over the past eighty years or so …Today, cultural honour survives only in a degraded form, in places where the official socialising process is weakest, as among urban gangs.
>
> (Bowman 2006: 6–7)

Constant exposure to other cultures and religions often contributed to containing and suppressing long-standing customary codes centred on the concepts of honour and revenge. For the Konyaks, one of the largest Naga ethnic groups living in the mountainous state of Nagaland, in North-East India, the prolonged contact with Christian missionaries progressively eroded the robustness of previous customs, including the once wide-spread practice of blood revenge—locally known as "headhunting." As explained by an ethnic Konyak, the conversion to Christianity embraced by the vast majority of the indigenous population inhibited the desire to seek vengeance to right a wrong: "We don't engage in blood feud because the belief is that Christ has forgiven our sins. The Konyaks were blanched into a completely new mindset, and this immensely contributed to them moving away from headhunting and tattooing" (Khan 2021). The last recorded episode of blood revenge taking place amongst the Konyaks dates to 1983 when a converted king exacted a revenge killing on the murderer of his uncle to put "a full stop to the perpetual cycle of shame" (Chopy 2021).

In Western Europe, the rise of the self-controlled individual occurred at a slower, but more sequential pace. Activated by the process of state centralisation and the decline of the culture of honour, the societal rejection of blood revenge came to completion during the first half of the 20th century, when defending one's honour with violence ceased being considered as a socially acceptable behaviour. As argued by Spierenburg (2008: 9), in European countries, the basis of male honour slowly but inexorably "drifted away from its close association with the body. Honour gradually became associated with inner virtue. Consequently, the need to employ violence in order to save one's face when insulted or challenged greatly diminished."

Defined by the author as "the spiritualisation of honour," the socio-cultural transition from a culture of violence to one of restraint com-pelled individuals not only to abstain from seeking retribution, but also to desire being seen as capable of exercising full control over their impulses. According to Shoemaker (2001: 207), in 18th-century London, this process was catalysed by the emergence of a new social code of politeness that, "with its expectations of affable and refined sociability for those aspiring to gentility, created a new, more restrained standard of public behaviour." Enfeebled by the stigmatisation of self-help justice, the residual vestiges of blood revenge were cast aside when millions of men were sent to fight and die in the trenches of the First World War (1914–1918). After returning from the frontlines, explains Nye (1998: 93), those who experienced the carnage of combat "had proven their courage in the face of far greater dangers, and those who had avoided service, or were too young to fight, could not hope to equal their ordeals in duelling-ground heroics."

The Legacy of Blood Revenge in Modern Society

The endurance of the principles underpinning the logic of blood revenge is typically found in societies that have rejected retaliatory violence as an acceptable means of settling interpersonal and inter-communal disputes. Despite ceasing to be a regulatory mechanism for society at large, the logic of blood revenge survives in the everyday interactions occurring between and within socially deviant communities, among which the most important are the Italian criminal organisations known as *Mafias*.

Existing and operating outside the boundaries of legality, *Mafias* developed alternative regulatory mechanisms, heavily informed by notions of honour and retaliation, derived from cultural values once prevalent amongst the populations living in Southern Italy—the birthplace of Italy's criminal organisations (Dickie 2005). By branding themselves as *uomini d'onore* (men of honour) and re-elaborating the customary precepts ingrained in the Southern Italian traditional "code of honour," *Mafiosi* prolonged the existence of codes otherwise eroded in nowadays' Italian society (Travaglino & Abrams 2019: 87). Among others, the custom of *vendetta* (blood revenge) is one of the most iconic practices of Mafia families and clans. In an underground world in which the family's name constitutes the "identity card" of a true "man of honour," an insult to one's reputation must be washed away with the blood of its perpetrator according to the informal tenet *sangue chiama sangue* (blood calls for blood) (Angeli 1998: 53).

As with more traditional variants of blood revenge, a *Mafioso* who fails to restore his family's damaged reputation experiences severe repercussions. This was the case of a repented *Mafioso* who, stigmatised as a coward by his relatives, could no longer accept the shame and ultimately carried out his revenge:

> [the person] was forced to suffer the never-ending disdain of his aunt and grandmother, who called him *infame* [derogatory term for "turncoat *Mafioso*"] because reluctant to avenge his grandfather. Under the unbearable social pressure, he had no choice but to satisfy their wishes.
>
> (Lo Baido et al. 2013: 98)

Although reminiscent of Southern Italian customs, revenge assassinations performed by *Mafiosi* have gone a long way from the tightly regulated modalities underpinning *blood* revenge killings. In contrast with their institutionalised predecessor, Mafia-related vendettas do not respond to the principle of individuality, do not respect the requirement of selectiveness, and abide by different concepts of equivalency. As a late 19th-century report to the Italian government specifies, during retaliatory raids, the *Mafioso* "is never alone: he is always supported by one of his close kinsmen—his sons in most cases" (Damiani 1885: 435). This is still the case for nowadays *Mafiosi*, as exemplified by the retaliatory raid carried out by a commando of armed men against a rival leader in a Southern Italian city in 2017 (Sánchez 2017). Within this new format of revenge killings, *any* relative—and not just the male agnates of the culprit—can be considered as a viable target of a revenge murder.

Defined in Mafia jargon as *vendetta trasversale* (transversal vengeance), the retaliatory attack can be directed against the culprit's wife and children if the *infame* is hiding under the state's protection. While it is not rare to see wives and daughters of direct culprits falling victim to revenge murders, children are increasingly becoming collateral or intentional targets of vendettas—which often claim the lives of any other person unfortunate enough to be with the target during the retaliatory raid (Pickering-Iazzi 2019; Parri 2014).

Once circumscribed to the territories where the *Mafias* have long been operating, the emigration of thousands of Italians during the last two centuries contributed to spreading the practice to other countries, where honour-related retributive killings have been on the rise. While vendettas traceable to Italian *Mafiosi* routinely occur in areas where the concentration of Italian immigrants is high, such as across parts of Australia (Sutton 2016) and Canada (Palumbo 2017), the increasing porosity of interstate borders is allowing numerous *Mafiosi* to chase down their targets abroad, as epitomised by the shootout that left six Italian mobsters dead in a German restaurant in 2007 (Euronews 2007). Although rooted in the traditional principles of honour, masculinity, and retaliation, this "new" form of revenge no longer adheres to the rules that once limited its endemic potential for violence, hence threatening to scale up the figures of innocents killed during retaliatory raids. At times of war, the emergence of a "culture of retaliation" based on modern remnants of eroded customary codes can prompt avengers to join armed groups and seek retaliation during high-risk collective action. The violent mobilisation of avengers adhering to unregulated retaliatory practices shapes, in turn, several key dynamics of irregular conflicts, which are described in more details in Chapter 5.

References

Akyol, Mustafa. "Where the Powerful Can Kill the Weak, as Long as They Pay," *CATO Institute*, June 30, 2020. Available at: www.cato.org/commentary/where-powerful-can-kill-weak-long-they-pay

Angeli, Francesco. *La Mafia Dentro: Psicologia e Psicopatologia di un Fondamentalismo* (Milan: FrancoAngeli, 1998). ISBN: 8846404084.

Barber, Kristie. "A Study of the Strength of Tribal Ties Among Rural and Urban Zanzibaris in Oman," *SIT Oman*, 2007. Available at: https://digitalcomm ons.macalester.edu/cgi/viewcontent.cgi?referer=&httpsredir=1&article=1003&context=macabroad

Bedford [pseudonym]. "The Disappearance of the Duel from English Life," *The Contemporary Review* 156, 1939: 217–224.

Bowman, James. "Decline of the Honor Culture," *Policy Review*, August–September 2009: 27–39. Available at: www.hoover.org/research/decline-honor-culture

Bowman, James. *Honor: A History* (New York: Encounter Books, 2006). ISBN: 1-59403-198-3.

Brown, Keith. The Extent and Nature of Feuding in Scotland, 1573–1625. PhD Thesis, University of Glasgow, 1983. http://theses.gla.ac.uk/id/eprint/3985

Byock, L. Jesse. "Feuding in Viking-Age Iceland's Great Village," in *Conflict in Medieval Europe: Changing Perspectives on Society and Culture*, edited by Brown, Warren C. and Górecki, Piotr (Aldershot: Ashgate, 2003), 228–241. ISBN: 9781315259666.

Cedoca. *Blood Feuds in Contemporary Albania: Characterisation, Prevalence and Response by the State.* June 29, 2017. Available at: www.cgrs.be/en/country-information/blood-feuds-contemporary-albania-characterisation-prevalence-and-response-state

Celik, Ayse & Shkreli, Alma. "An Analysis of Reconciliatory Mediation in Northern Albania: The Role of Customary Mediators," *Europe-Asia Studies* 62(6), 2010: 885–914. DOI: 10.1080/09668136.2010.489253

Center for Human Rights in Iran. "How Many Camels Is One Human Life Worth? Attorney Calls for Reform in Iran's "Blood Money" Scheme." December 14, 2017. Available at www.iranhumanrights.org/2017/12/how-many-camels-is-one-human-life-worth-attorney-calls-for-reform-in-irans-blood-money-scheme/

Chaoul, Melhem. "Clan Violence in Lebanon's Bekaa Brings Back Memories of Civil War," *The National*, November 24, 2020. Available at: www.pressreader.com/uae/the-national-news/20201124/281552293409077

Chopy, G. Kanato. *Christianity and Politics in Tribal India* (Albany: State University of New York Press, 2021). ISBN: 9781438485836.

Dalby, Michael. "Revenge and the Law in Traditional China," *The American Journal of Legal History* 25(4), 1981: 267–307. DOI: 10.2307/845275.

Damiani, Abele. *Atti della Giunta per la Inchiesta Agraria e Sulle Condizioni della Classe Agricola* (Rome: Forzani e C., 1885).

Deeb, Mary-Jane. "The Society and Its Environment" in *Algeria: A Country Study*, edited by Metz, C. Helen (Richmond: Department of the Army, 1994), 67–126. ISBN: 084440831X.

Dickie, John. *Cosa Nostra: A History of the Sicilian Mafia* (New York: Palgrave MacMillan, 2005). ISBN: 1403970424.

Durkheim, Émile. *Professional Ethics and Civic Morals* (London: Routledge, 1992 [1957]).

Durkheim, Émile. *The Division of Labour in Society* (London: The MacMillan Press, 1984 [1893]).Elias, Norbert. *The Civilizing Process: Sociogenetic and Psychogenetic Investigations* (Malden: Blackwell Publishing, 2013).

Euronews. "Vendetta Killings: The Mafia's Long Reach from Italy," August 15, 2007. Available at: www.euronews.com/2007/08/15/vendetta-killings-the-mafia-s-long-reach-from-italy

Favali, Lyda & Paterman, Roy. *Blood, Land, and Sex: Legal and Political Pluralism in Eritrea* (Bloomington: Indiana University Press, 2003). ISBN: 9780253342058.

Frost, Peter & d'Anglure, Bernard. "Western Europe, State Formation, and Genetic Pacification," *Evolutionary Psychology* 13(1), 2015: 230–243. DOI: 10.1177/147470491501300114

Gallant, Thomas. "Creating 'Western Civilization' on a Greek Island" in *Experiencing Dominion: Culture, Identity, and Power in the British Mediterranean*, edited by Gallant, Thomas (Notre Dame: University of Notre Dame Press, 2002), 57–74. ISBN: 9780268028015.

Gallant, Thomas. "Honor, Masculinity, and Ritual Knife Fighting in Nineteenth-Century Greece," *The American Historical Review* 105(2), 2000: 359–382. DOI: 10.1086/ahr/105.2.359

Gazso, Amber & McDaniel, A. Susan. "Families by Choice and the Management of Low Income Through Social Supports," *Journal of Family Issues* 36(3), 2015: 371–395. DOI: 10.1177/0192513X13506002

Giorgi, Chiara. "Magistrati d'Oltremare," *Studi Storici* 51(4), 2010: 855–879. DOI: 10.7375/70278

Gordon, Robert. "Some Notes Towards Understanding the Dynamics of Blood Money" in *Homicide Compensation in Papua New Guinea: Problems and Prospects*, edited by Scaglion, Richard (Papua New Guinea: Law Reform Commission of Papua New Guinea, 1981). ISBN: 0724707301.

Gould, V. Roger. "Revenge as Sanction and Solidarity Display: An Analysis of Vendettas in Nineteenth-Century Corsica," *American Sociological Review* 65(5), 2000: 682–704. DOI: 10.2307/2657542

Government of Canada. "Issue Paper: Albania Blood Feuds." *Immigration and Refugee Board of Canada*, May 2008. Available at:www.ecoi.net/en/file/local/1148361/1684_1243258524_http-www2-irb-cisr-gc-ca-en-research-publi cations-index-e-htm.pdf

Grutzpalk, Jonas. "Blood Feud and Modernity: Max Weber's and Émile Durkheim's Theories," *Journal of Classical Sociology* 2(2), 2002: 115–134. DOI: 10.1177/1468795X02002002854

Hassanein, S. Ahmed. "The Impact of Islamic Criminal Law on the Qatari Penal Code," *Arab Law Quarterly* 32(1), 2018: 60–79. DOI: 10.1163/15730255-12314 037

Herzfeld, Michael. *The Poetics of Manhood: Contest and Identity in a Cretan Mountain Village* (Princeton: Princeton University Press, 1988). ISBN: 978-0691102443.

Hosken, Andrew & Kasapi, Albana. "The Children Trapped by Albania's Blood Feuds," *BBC News*, November 12, 2017. Available at: www.bbc.com/news/world-europe-41901300

Jalabadze, Natia. "The Resurgence of Blood Feud in the Georgian Lowlands," *Caucasus Analytical Digest* 42(30), September 30, 2012: 7–9. Available at: https://css.ethz.ch/en/publications/cad/cad-all-issues-and-articles/details.html?id=/t/h/e/r/the_resurgence_of_blood_feud_in_the_geor

Jalabadze, Natia & Janiashvili, Lavrenti. "Traditional Law and Blood Feud: Svan Legal Practice in Soviet Times and in Contemporary Southern Georgia" in *State and Legal Practice in the Caucasus*, edited by Voell, Stéphane & Kaliszewska, Iwona (New York: Routledge, 2016), 37–49. ISBN: 9780367599584.

Janiashvili, Lavrenti. "Traditional Legal Practice in Soviet Times," in *Traditional Law in the Caucasus*, edited by Voell, Stéphane (Bamberg: Curupira, 2016), 83–124. ISBN: 978-3-8185-0524-0.

Khan, Arman. "The Fading Tattoo Traditions of India's Last Headhunters," *Vice News*, November 17, 2021. Available at: www.vice.com/en/article/qjb8bb/headhunters-tribe-nagaland-india-traditional-tattoo-tradition

Larmer, Brook. "Medieval Mountain Hideaway," *National Geographic*, October 2014. Available at: www.nationalgeographic.com/magazine/article/svanetia-georgia-caucasus-mountains

Lawson, Colin & Saltmarshe, Douglas. "Security and Economic Transition: Evidence from North Albania," *Europe-Asia Studies* 52(1), 2000: 133–148. DOI: https://doi.org/10.1080/09668130098307

Lendon, Jon. "Homeric Vengeance and the Outbreak of Greek Wars" in *War and Violence in Ancient Greece*, edited by van Wees, Hans (Swansea: The Classical Press of Wales, 2000), 1–30. ISBN: 0715630466.

Lo Baido, Rosa; La Grutta, Sabrina & Di Blasi, Marie. "Sequestrati dalla Vendetta: 'Rimanere Chiusi Fuori dall'Oggetto'," *Narrare i Gruppi* 13(1), 2013: 91–101.

Lorentzen, Håkon & Hustinx, Lesley. "Civic Involvement and Modernization," *Journal of Civil Society* 3(2), 2007: 101–118. DOI: 10.1080/17448680701554282

Mazzette, Antonietta; Bussu, Anna; Patrizi, Patrizia; Pulino, Daniele & Tidore, Camillo. *La Criminalità in Sardegna. Reati, autori e incidenza sul territorio* (Sassari: Centro di Studi Urbani Università di Sassari, 2011). Available at: https://dissuf.uniss.it/sites/st11/files/oscrim/ii_rapporto_di_ricerca.pdf

Medzhid, Faik. "Blood Feuds Turns Out to Be a Modern Trend in Azerbaijan," *Caucasian Knot*, August 1, 2019. Available at: www.eng.kavkaz-uzel.eu/artic les/47989/

Meydan TV. "V for Vendetta: Blood Feuds in Azerbaijan—A Thing of the Past?" *Meydan TV*, July 31, 2019. Available at: www.meydan.tv/en/article/v-vende tta-blood-feuds-azerbaijan-are-they-thing-past/

Miller, I. William. "In Defense of Revenge" in *Medieval Crime and Social Control*, edited by Hanawalt, A. Barbara & Wallace, Davvid (Minneapolis: University of Minnesota Press, 1999), 70–89. ISBN: 9780816631698.

Mills, D. "Kataki-Uchi: The Practice of Blood-Revenge in Pre-Modern Japan," *Modern Asian Studies* 10(4), 1976: 525–542. www.jstor.org/stable/311761

Mustafa, Mentor & Young, Antonia. "Feud Narratives: Contemporary Deployments of Kanun in Shala Valley, Northern Albania," *Anthropological Notebook* 14(2), 2008: 87–107. ISSN 1408-032X.

Nuttall, Mark. "Power and Kinship in Shuar and Achuar Society" in *Dividends of Kinship: Meanings and Uses of Social Relatedness*, edited by Schweitzer, P. Peter (London: Routledge, 2000), 61–92. ISBN: 0415182840.

Nye, Robert. "The End of Modern French Duel" in *Men and Violence: Gender, Honor and Rituals in Modern Europe and America (The History of Crime & Criminal Justice)*, edited by Spierenburg, Pieter (Ohio: The Ohio State University Press, 1998), 82–95. ISBN: 0814207529.

Palumbo, Jessica. "'Revenge Doesn't Have a Statute of Limitations': Mafia Expert on Musitano Killing," *CBC*, May 4, 2017. Available at: www.cbc.ca/news/can ada/hamilton/revenge-doesn-t-have-a-statute-of-limitations-mafia-expert-on-musitano-killing-1.4098896

Parri, Tom. "Children Murdered by the Mafia as Italian Mobsters Sink to New Low," *Mirror*, April 12, 2014. Available at: www.mirror.co.uk/news/world-news/children-murdered-mafia-italian-mobsters-3402712

Pascoe, Daniel. "Is Diya a Form of Clemency?" *Boston University International Law Journal* 34(149), 2016: 150–179. Available at: https://scholars.cityu.edu. hk/en/publications/is-diya-a-form-of-clemency(5d0f64da-6fb8-4a3e-b388-a76d8c931214).html

Pickering-Iazzi, Robin. *Dead Silent: Life Stories of Girls and Women Killed by the Italian Mafias, 1878–2019* (University of Wisconsin Milwaukee [UWM] French, Italian and Comparative Literature Faculty Books, 2019). Available at: https://dc.uwm.edu/freita_facbooks/2

Plaku, Vilma; Bosna, Vittoria & Grattigliano, Ignazio. "The Kanun as a Self-Governance Code in Italian-Albanian Criminal Contexts: A Research Conducted in the Republic of Albania," *Clin Ter* 170(6), 2019: 435–447. DOI: 10.7417/CT.2019.2173

Pollock, B. Frederick & Maitland, W. Frederic. *The History of English Law Before the Time of Edward I* (New Jersey: The Lawbook Exchange, 2009 [1898]). ISBN: 0865977526.

Raggio, Osvaldo. "Etnografia e Storia Politica. La Faida e il Caso della Corsica," *Quaderni Storici* 25(75), 1990: 937–954. www.jstor.org/stable/43778206

Ratelle, Jean-François & Souleimanov, A. Emil. "Retaliation in Rebellion: The Missing Link to Explaining Insurgent Violence in Dagestan," *Terrorism and Political Violence* 29(4), 2017: 573–592. DOI: 10.1080/09546553.2015.1005076

Sánchez, Gonzalo. "The Forgotten Foggian Mafia Strikes Terror in Southern Italy," *Agencia EFE*, August 11, 2017. Available at: www.efe.com/efe/english/varios/the-forgotten-foggian-mafia-strikes-terror-in-southern-italy/50000269-3349707

Shoemaker, Robert. "Male Honor and the Decline of Public Violence in Eighteenth-Century London," *Social History* 26(2), 2001: 190–208. DOI: 10.1080/03071020110041352

Spierenburg, Pieter. *A History of Murder: Personal Violence in Europe from the Middle Ages to the Present* (Cambridge: Polity Press, 2008). ISBN: 978–0745643786.

Sutton, Candice. "I'm Going to Cut His "F★★★in" Head off," *Mail Online*, January 31, 2016. Available at: www.dailymail.co.uk/news/article-3400577/How-31-Calabrian-mafia-families-control-60-percent-Australia-s-drug-trade.html

Tepshi, Aferdita. "Blood Feuds and Revenge in Canons and Medieval Statues and Social Consequences," *Academic Journal of Interdisciplinary Studies* 4(3), 2015: 199–206. DOI:10.5901/ajis.2015.v4n3p199

Travaglino, Giovanni & Abrams, Dominic. "How Criminal Organisations Exert Secret Power over Communities: An Intracultural Appropriation Theory of Cultural Values and Norms." *European Review of Social Psychology* 30(1), 2019: 74–122. DOI: 10.1080/10463283.2019.1621128

Weber, Max. *Economy and Society: An Outline of Interpretive Sociology*, edited by Roth, Guenther & Wittich, Claus (Berkeley: University of California Press, 1978 [1922]). ISBN: 978-0520035003.

Weber, Max. "Politics as a Vocation" in *From Max Weber: Essays in Sociology*, edited by Gerth, H. Hans & Mills, C. Wright. (New York: Oxford University Press, 1946 [1921]), 77–128. ISBN: 9780415482691.

Wilson, Stephen. *Feuding, Conflict and Banditry in Nineteenth-Century Corsica* (Cambridge: Cambridge University Press, 2002). ISBN: 978-0521522649.

Wormald, Jenny. "Bloodfeud, Kindred and Government in Early Modern Scotland," *Past & Present* 87, 1980: 54–97. DOI: 10.1093/past/87.1.54

Wu, John. "Reading from Ancient Chinese Codes and Other Sources of Chinese Law and Legal Ideas," *Michigan Law Review* 19(5), 1921: 502–536. Available at: https://repository.law.umich.edu/mlr/vol19/iss5/3

4   The Role of Blood Revenge in Irregular Warfare

Although the role of blood revenge in irregular warfare is rather overlooked in the security studies literature, a series of influential works from different academic fields provide important insights into the logic of culturally driven retaliatory practices in wartime. Studies on revenge in international politics shed light on the role played by honour, humiliation, and shame in triggering and prolonging wars, further showing that societies where a culture of honour endures are more prone to endorse military aggression as a status-restoring practice. Looking at the micro-dimension of political violence, scholars of gender studies further demonstrated that male honour and warrior ethos are often key drivers of violent mobilisation in societies where the penchant for revenge is engrained in the local sociocultural milieu.

Grounding the study of blood revenge in the wider social science literature allows for a more robust analysis of the impact blood revenge in warfare, further identifying the contexts in which it holds little to no relevance. This is particularly important for the study of interstate conflicts. Although these conflicts are usually defined by regular (or conventional) warfare, forms of hybrid and irregular warfare nonetheless occur at a subterranean level and can be influenced by blood revenge. In dozens of past and present interstate conflicts, including the ongoing war in Ukraine, partisan units, pro-government militias, and foreign fighters take part in the combat operations, adding a dimension of irregular warfare beneath the dynamics of conventional warfighting. As some of the fighters serving in these units may be driven into mobilisation by blood revenge, such as some pro-Kyiv Chechen militants, exploring the dynamics of interstate conflicts captures an important, yet under-explored dimension of the topics covered in this book. In the following section, we provide a comprehensive overview of the relevant social science literature, drawing upon different streams of research to set the stage for an in-depth analysis of the ways in which blood revenge shapes irregular warfare.

DOI: 10.4324/9781003387527-4

Situating Blood Revenge in the Social Science Literature

Revenge in International Relations

Drawing upon ethnographic reports from 90 societies across the globe, Ross (1986) was arguably the first to claim that a society's overall conflict level is rooted in psycho-cultural dispositions to aggression. His cross-cultural theory of political conflict and violence, with its focus on retaliatory behaviours, inspired a new stream of research into the role of cultural factors during the inception, course, and aftermath of conflicts. Marking a departure from previous foreign policy models based on rational-choice theory, Harkavy (2000: 345) set up a research agenda on the interconnections between humiliation and revenge, arguing that the collective rage resulting from national defeat activates an "almost ineradicable need for vengeance."

Pushing forward Harkavy's work, Löwenheim and Heimann (2008) advanced the first conceptualisation of revenge in international politics. Drawing upon evidence from the 2006 Second Israel–Hezbollah War, the two authors inductively show that a state is more likely to resort to retaliatory cross-border force when the previous harm is perceived as morally outrageous, the humiliation arising from the event flares in intensity, and the international norms governing the use of retaliatory violence are loosely institutionalised. Building on previous discoveries, Bernhart's (2016, 2021) recent works provide an important contribution to the study of humiliation, revenge, and conflict. In a seminal article published in *Security Studies*, Bernhart (2016) argues that humiliated and disrespected states are more prone to engage in competitive status-seeking behaviour to reassert their position in the international area, even when doing so comes at steep material and strategic costs. He intriguingly argues that the so-called Scramble for Africa, which occurred amongst great powers at the end of the 19th century, was partly driven by the desire to wash away the humiliation of previous defeats through expensive practices of territorial expansion.

The importance that states assign to their reputational status is not solely circumscribed to the arena of interstate wars. In a thought-provoking study on the psychology of humiliation in asymmetric conflicts, McCauley hypothesises that the acts of terrorism can cause international humiliation to powerful countries, in the same way that states are capable of shaming non-state actors with lethal force, as was the case with the killing of Al-Qaeda's leader Osama Bin Laden by the U.S. special forces in May 2011. "This symmetry," McCauley (2017: 263) argues, "makes humiliation the prototypical emotional experience of asymmetric conflicts." These findings suggest that the desire to retaliate for a perceived insult or loss of prestige is often a strong motivating factor for the recourse to interstate violence—a dynamic that closely resembles the dynamics that drive individuals to engage in retributive violence as a status-restoring practice. Although the behaviour of states can be explained by a myriad of other theories of international relations, these studies indicate that cultural beliefs on what constitutes an appropriate response to shame and humiliation can constitute important "apolitical" drivers for violence not only for individuals but also for societies as well.

Other scholars have investigated the connection between cultural attitudes to violence and the state's response to national humiliation. In her volume of *Vengeful Citizens, Violent States*, Stein (2019) looks at the micro-foundations of international violence, arguing that vengeful populations will be more supportive of the use of force when that use of force is framed as punishment for a perceived wrong. Specifically, she finds in elected leaders the missing link between individual vengefulness and state violence, persuasively arguing that "citizens' desire for revenge against an adversary is a potent force that national leaders can mobilise into support for war by using strategically crafted rhetoric that frames the use of force as a punishment the adversary deserves to suffer" (Ibid.: 2). Similarly, Dafoe and Caughey (2016) compared the conflict behaviour of the United States when the country was led by presidents raised in the South, where the culture of honour is stronger, with its behaviour when led by non-Southerners. Their results show that militarised interstate disputes occurring under Southerner presidents have been "twice as likely to involve the use of force, have lasted on average twice as long, and have been three times as likely to be won by the United States" (Ibid.: 371). It follows that presidents who are more concerned with reputation are less likely to back down once the United States is drawn into an interstate dispute, much like any individual who, coming from a culture of honour, feels duty-bound to engage in violence as an honour-restoring practice. These studies show that, in societies where a culture of honour endures, the desire to engage in retributive violence to defend and restore honour is a far more important and compelling driver of collective behaviour than what many scholars have so far surmised.

Revenge and Gender in Political Violence

Research into the social role of gender provides further insights into how concepts of honour and masculinity drive the penchant for revenge. Drawing upon survey data collected from high school students in the

United States and aggregated over 20 years, Brown et al. (2009) found that states where the culture of honour is prominent had more than twice as many school shootings per capita as states where cultural concepts of honour are absent, suggesting that males from the former areas are more prone to engage in aggressive retaliatory responses to perceived insults and humiliations. Similarly, Bjarnegård et al. (2019: 7152) used micro-level survey data from Thailand to demonstrate that political activists who experienced family-of-origin violence are more likely to engage in political violence "due to the diffusion of masculine honour ideology and violence norms, whereby violence is seen as a just, appropriate, and masculine response to conflict."

Building on these studies, Tschantret (2020) carried out a multilevel statistical analysis of domestic terrorist attacks in the United States from 1970 to 2015, finding that terrorism is deadlier in the South, where the culture of honour is more deeply ingrained. According to the author, terrorists from honour cultures are "more likely to attempt unrestrained attacks to reaffirm their reputations as decisively as possible," usually through acts of indiscriminate violence against groups associated with the perceived offender (Ibid.: 331). Similar findings emerge from interviews carried out by Speckhard and Ahkmedova (2006a) with relatives of Chechen suicide terrorists, who consistently referred to honour and revenge as primary motivating factors for their loved ones' mobilisation into extremist armed groups. Correspondingly, cross-cultural statistical data shows that inter-group aggressions are more likely to take place in cultures of honour, where warriors who have proven themselves in combat enjoy higher levels of social rewards (Nawata 2020, see also Cao et al. 2021).

Although women in cultures of honour are typically exempt from acting as avengers, the collective traumatisation experienced at times of war can erode the rigidity of traditional gender roles. Studies conducted on Chechen and Iraqi female suicide bombers suggest that women living in cultures of honour may be willing to step in as avengers, engaging in acts of retaliatory violence on behalf of a close male relative, such as a husband or a son, killed by a belligerent faction (Speckhard 2009; Speckhard & Ahkmedova 2006b). Shedding light on the cultural dynamics of gendered violence, this bulk of literature adds a much-needed new perspective on how acts of honour-restoring violence are legitimised and perpetrated amid an armed conflict.

Blood Revenge in the Political Science Literature

Finally, a body of scholarship has zoomed in on the role of blood revenge in inter-group struggles. From an examination of 19th-century court documents from the Mediterranean island of Corsica, Gould (1999) finds that blood revenge escalates to the form of collective violence when the kinsmen of a warring individual get involved in the dispute despite the risk of violent escalation. Evidence shows that failure to prevent escalation compels members of the injured party to violently mobilise and reassert their group solidarity vis-à-vis their adversaries. Drawing upon evidence from the Cambodian genocide of 1975–1979, Hinton (1998) found that the local cultural model of disproportionate retaliation, dubbed "a head for an eye," incentivised countless Cambodians to exact blood revenge upon members of antagonistic groups, thus aggravating the range and scope of massacres.

Although anthropological accounts pay much attention to vendettas and blood feuds as important drivers of inter-group conflicts, political scientists have, with a few notable exceptions, neglected to consider their role in asymmetric conflicts. Souleimanov and Aliyev (2015a) were arguably the first to discuss the role of blood revenge as a vehicle of violent mobilisation in civil wars. Drawing upon data collected during interviews with former insurgents and eyewitnesses of the Russian–Chechen Wars, the authors showed that the compelling obligation to exact blood revenge pushed thousands of apolitical Chechens to seek membership in rebel bands against the Russian forces.

The findings of this initial work inspired a follow-up study by Souleimanov et al. (2022a) , which advances the first research agenda for the role of blood revenge in civil war. Broadening the cross-case qualitative evidence available on the topic with a newly compiled dataset, the authors argue that blood revenge shape several key dynamics of civil wars, namely the processes of violent mobilisation, target selection, recruitment, defection, and disengagement. Their quantitative data shows that, between 1971 and 2021, two-thirds of all civil wars have occurred in countries where blood revenge endures. Furthermore, civil wars occurring in areas with an active tradition of blood revenge registered twice as many battle fatalities and were almost four times more likely to end up in a stalemate, five times more likely to be ongoing, and almost twice as likely to drag on as low-intensity conflicts. In mapping the global impact of blood revenge, the study provides a novel systematisation of long-ignored aspects of irregular conflicts, challenging conventional wisdom on civil wars, and showing that the root causes of rebel violence may oftentimes be intrinsically cultural, rather than ideological or opportunistic.

Building on the extant scholarship and drawing upon evidence from different areas of the world, this chapter advances a concise overview of the ways in which blood revenge shapes irregular warfare. Setting the stage for the upcoming discussion in Chapter 5, the following sections address the main aspects of blood revenge in irregular warfare, specifically the patterns of (a) violent mobilisation, (b) target selection, and (c) recruitment and disengagement.

Violent Mobilisation

The global understanding of what motivates people to take part in forms of high-risk armed resistance has long been informed by Olson's (1965 [1971]) framework on the collective action problem faced by belligerents in civil wars. Since the goal of any rebel group is to achieve *collective* goods that are nonrival and nonexcludable, the best choice for a rational individual is to stay neutral and enjoy the benefits achieved by others willing to bear the costs of active participation.[1] As remarked by Kalyvas and Kocher (2007: 181), "the ills of civil war, death of self and family, economic collapse, and forced relocation" are compelling enough reasons for individuals to "free ride" on rebellion.

When it comes to cultures of honour, however, free riding is hardly ever an individual's preferred course of action. In societies where honour and dishonour "provide the currency" of social stance, choosing to leave an affront unavenged is tantamount to leaving one's honour in a state of moral desecration (Pitt-Rivers 2013). As explained by an elderly Pashtun from the tribal areas of Pakistan, each tribesman is required to monitor the behaviour of his peers, applying the appropriate social sanctions whenever a prospective avenger fails in his task: "A *nar* (masculine) and *gheratmand* (honourable) *sare* (man) is generally thought as a person who does not tolerate but avenges … otherwise people consider us a *begherat* [dishonourable man] … which is unbearable … like *zwande marg de* (a living death) for a Pakhtun" (Saeed 2012: 112). Given that the stains of honour can only be cleansed through the act of blood revenge, a prospective avenger who free rides on his social obligations will typically face unsurmountable social sanctions for an action deemed as irrational and socially despicable. As a former Chechen insurgent put it, "we simply had no other choice but to take our blood [revenge], even if we knew we'd lose our lives and risk the lives of our kin" (Souleimanov & Aliyev 2017: 49). Therefore, in theatres of irregular warfare, blood revenge provides a local solution to the collective action problem faced by insurgents and pro-government militias alike, which receive steady inflows of volunteers motivated by the desire of exacting vengeance against their enemies (Souleimanov et al. 2022a).

For many of these avengers, the compelling obligation to restore their family's honour through vengeance comes irrespective of one's political or economic interests. In fact, violent mobilisation driven by blood revenge finds its triggers in *apolitical* motives, typically revolving around the need to avenge episodes of murder, rape, severe injuries, or insults inflicted upon the avenger himself or any of their close kinsmen. Personal grievances, anger, and frustration may also motivate the avenger to speed up the process of violent mobilisation. For a teenage boy from the Afghan province of Helmand, the decision to join the ranks of the Afghan Local Police along with his brother was chiefly motivated by their quest to exact revenge on the Taliban for the death of their father: "The enemy killed my father, so I am also fighting" (Rasmussen 2016). A century before, in 1916, two brothers belonging to the "Blood Indians," an indigenous community from the Canadian region of Southern Alberta, enlisted in the Canadian Expeditionary Force (CEF) to exact blood revenge for their father, killed in the trenches of World War I in November 1915 (Mountain Horse 1979: 140). In the two cases presented, the decision to participate in the hostilities responds to the customary obligation of blood revenge; yet it also shows that personal grievances and a desire for retribution may also act as catalysers for the violent mobilisation of avengers. In fact, the two are often interwoven, so much so that it may be challenging even for the avenger himself to tell the two apart (Souleimanov & Colombo 2021: 72).

Stories of avengers driven by sociocultural codes and a personal desire for vengeance emerge from dozens of conflicts that occurred in areas where blood revenge endures. In the 1970s, the outbreak of internecine conflict in Mindanao, the second-largest island in the Philippines, contributed to pushing dozens of apolitical individuals into the ranks of local armed rebels. As recalled by a close relative of a rebel fighter, the atrocities inflicted upon the population drove the penchant for payback, known in the local language as *rido*:

> During those days, the Ilagas [Filipino Christian militia] and the military threatened our lives... I remember several people died in our family and in the community including innocent children. I told myself when I grow up, I want to continue fighting the *satru* (unbelievers) so I can avenge the deaths of my people.
>
> (Conciliation Resources 2016: 44)

In Nigeria, the mobilisation of young men into the ranks of progovernment militias was largely driven by the compelling obligation to avenge the deaths of their loved ones. As reported by a group of researchers in 2014, the establishment of anti-jihadist paramilitaries in north-eastern Nigeria was made possible by the enlistment of highly motivated avengers:

In many cases, especially at the beginning of the group's formation, new recruits joined the Civilian JTF [Joint Task Force] to avenge the deaths of family members, who had been killed at the hands of JAS [Jama'atu Ahlis Sunna Lidda'awati wal-Jihad, the then local al-Qaeda affiliate colloquially known as Boko Haram].

(Watch List 2014: 29)

The same pathway to violent mobilisation was experienced by a rebel fighter from Guadalcanal, an island situated in the Solomon Islands archipelago, which was engulfed from 1999 to 2003 in a bloody civil war fought between the nationalist Isatabu Freedom Movement (IFM), formerly known as Guadalcanal Revolutionary Army (GRA), and the Malaita Eagle Force (MEF), a paramilitary force set up to defend the diasporic Malaitans living on the island. At first uninvested in the political dimension of the tensions between the two ethnic groups, the Malaitan man only took up arms when his father was captured and killed by GRA militants in 1998:

I was still in the police force at that time and I tried my best to find my father… Some people from Guadalcanal I knew said to me: 'Andrew, we saw your daddy blindfolded and taken away, he was killed'… From that situation, I decided that I should take up arms and become a militant.

(Solomon Islands Government 2012: 246)

The important role played by kinship ties is another common trait of most episodes of blood revenge–driven violent mobilisation. This is so because the social obligation of defending one's family or clan's honour does not simply cease because the appointed avenger fails to retaliate. As defending the family's honour is in every kinsman's best interest, the logic of blood revenge can often lead to the *collective* mobilisation of multiple blood relatives seeking to maximise their chances of succeeding in a revenge killing. In mid-2008, Lebanon's second largest city, Tripoli, was shaken by clashes that erupted between Sunni and Alawite residents. Following these clashes, a group of Sunni residents reportedly asked local jihadi groups to retaliate on their behalf. As a local Salafi sheikh put it at the time, "what happened in the capital [of the North Governorate] was a humiliation. Everyone is calling for revenge. Even our women are urging us to respond" (International Crisis Group 2010: 28).

At times of conflict, the mobilisation of avengers belonging to the same family, clan, or tribe sustains a self-enforcing cycle of revenge-driven violent mobilisation, which generates higher numbers of casualties and battle fatalities as the conflict drags on. For many avengers from the Kurdish-inhabited regions of Turkey, mobilising into local pro-government militias, colloquially known as Village Guards, offered an unmissable opportunity to settle long-simmering disputes with impunity. Formally established in 1985 to counter the Kurdistan Workers' Party (PKK), a local separatist insurgent group, the Village Guards' ranks were quickly filled with dozens of kinsmen who were seeking to gain an upper hand against their blood enemies. A famous case comes from the village of Bilge, in Southeastern Anatolia, where members of two families involved in a blood feud joined the Village Guards to obtain access to weapons, which were then used in a massacre that resulted in the deaths of 44 people in May 2009. As stated by a local government official at the time, "there was hostility between [the] Ari family and [the] Çelebi family. For the first time they bumped into each other in 1992. They became village guards in order to ensure the safety of their lives and carry their guns comfortably. Following that, the other side also became village guards" (Özar et al. 2013: 131).

In other cases, blood feuds between members of different militias dragged entire communities into cycles of escalatory tit-for-tat revenge attacks. As recalled by a Kurdish villager, clashes between members of rival families would often engulf dozens of clansmen into long-running blood feuds: "His father was held responsible for the [alleged] murder of seven village guards, and soon thereafter he was killed by another village guard from a different village... This incident started a blood feud between two villages. Berut's village was evacuated" (Biner 2012: 241). In such circumstances, traditional leaders may often be the only figures capable of de-escalating conflicts. When, in 1990, a Touk tribesman, a member of a Christian clan based in Eastern Lebanon, killed a member of the Shite clan of the Amhaz, the respective leaders averted the eruption of an all-out feud using traditional conflict resolution mechanisms. As explained by the victim's father, the decision of a clan leader to peacefully settle a dispute is final and binding for all parties: "Nothing could satisfy my thirst to ... avenge my son's blood, but this was a clan's decision and I willingly yield to it" (Saoud 1991).

In other cases, the collective trauma caused by war and violence prompted many to relinquish vengeance in favour of forgiveness. During the civil wars that took place in Liberia, the killing of innocent civilians pushed countless apolitical avengers into the arms of local militias. When several child soldiers were asked why they decided to take up arms and join a rebel faction, many pointed to the compelling desire to avenge their fallen relatives: "for revenge, because my papa was killed", "I saw NPFL [National Patriotic Front of Liberia] kill my mother in Upper

Lofa Country," and "AFL [Armed Forces of Liberia] killed my mother" (Human Rights Watch 1994: 12). After the war, personal vendettas subsided, with many families preferring peaceful legal settlements over the perpetuation of revenge. This was the case of a Christian family in Congo city, which decided not to pursue vengeance against the relatives of their teenage daughter's murderer, and rather sought satisfaction in legal courts: "We don't want blood for blood. We don't want any revenge. Our country has seen too much of that, we forgive, we require nothing" (Parley 2021).

For local authorities, the mobilisation of multiple avengers into the ranks of armed militias is often a source of concern, one that can inhibit the use of armed force to suppress armed militias. In February 2002, the U.S. government manifested its interest in eradicating a kidnap-for-ransom militant group operating in Basilan, an island located in the Philippines. Soon thereafter, representatives of the Moro National Liberation Front (MNLF) and Moro Islamic Liberation Front (MILF), the *de facto* authorities of the province, raised concerns over the risk of triggering blood feuds. As explained by a former MNLF operative, "This [operation] could backfire... If people get killed, their families will want revenge" (Murphy 2002). One way for states to de-escalate the risk of dragging multiple kinsmen into the arms of rebel groups is through the recourse to traditional conflict resolution mechanisms. When, in April 1979, troops belonging to the United Nations Interim Force in Lebanon (UNIFIL) killed two militants of the South Lebanon Army (SLA), a Christian-dominated Lebanese militia, the group's leader demanded monetary compensation to prevent the fallen militants' relatives and comrades-in-arms to declare a blood feud on UNIFIL. The warring sides were reportedly reconciled when UNIFIL paid the requested blood money, coming to terms with the SLA's leadership (Findlay 2002: 108).

Most of the blood feuds occurring amidst a conflict typically take place in areas relatively close to the avengers' place of residence, and in any case within the boundaries of their home countries. Nonetheless, the compelling obligation to exact blood revenge can motivate avengers to join armed groups engaged in foreign civil wars. This is the case of hundreds of North-Eastern Caucasians who, prevented from retaliating against their blood enemies in their home countries, chose to become foreign fighters in distant battlefields. When the Syrian Civil War broke out in 2011, scores of Chechen avengers joined Syrian jihadi groups for a chance to face Russian-backed forces in combat (Souleimanov 2014). As shown by a popular song shared on Chechen jihadi blogs at the time, the desire to exact revenge for the Russian brutalities was a potent incentive for joining the Syrian "Holy War": "I survived to be able to live;

I survived to be able to believe; I survived to be able to take revenge" (International Crisis Group 2016: 28).

For dozens of young Kists, an ethnic group of Chechen descent living on the Georgian side of the border with Chechnya, travelling to Syria was perceived as a once-in-a-lifetime opportunity for avenging their relatives killed during the Russian–Chechen Wars (Amashukely 2019: 23). Similarly, a foreign fighter from Dagestan reported that fighting in Syria, rather than in the Caucasus, would have prevented his relatives for becoming targets of the government's retribution: "I wanted to fight against the Russians and their puppets, but I would not jeopardise my entire family for that. But in Syria, you can fight your jihad … and you can even kill Russian soldiers" (Ratelle 2020: 65).

The Russian intervention in Ukraine offered another opportunity for avengers seeking to confront their blood enemies in combat. In 2014, the deployment of Chechen units in support of the pro-Russian local militias fighting in Eastern Ukraine prompted dozens of Chechen avengers to join the pro-Ukrainian camp for a chance to retaliate (Shuster 2015). The stream of Chechen avengers joining the fray in Ukraine registered an upsurge during the 2022 Russian invasion of Ukraine. As explained by a former Chechen jihadist who fought in Syria, the deployment of *Kadyrovtsy*, whose ranks are filled with pro-Russian paramilitary fighters controlled by Ramzan Kadyrov, head of the Chechen Republic, as part of the Russian invasion force motivated countless Chechens to become foreign fighters on the Ukrainian side: "*Kadyrovtsy* are in Ukraine fighting alongside the Russians, that makes it every Chechen man's responsibility to confront the enemies of Chechnya" (Prothero 2022).

The same holds true for numerous Syrians who sought to join the fray in Ukraine for a chance to retaliate against the Russians. As reported by a Syrian rebel, travelling to Ukraine would have offered a chance to face Russian soldiers in combat: "I have relatives held in Assad's prisons, and others who have been killed by Russian attacks must be avenged" (al-Aswad 2022). Correspondingly, for some Afghan immigrants residing in Ukraine at the time of the invasion, joining pro-Ukrainian militias offered an opportunity for avenging their grandparents who died during the Soviet–Afghan War of 1979–1989 (Latifi & Haris 2022). During an interview, a resident of Chagcharan, the capital of the Ghor Province in Northern Afghanistan, told that many locals wished to travel to Ukraine to fight the Russians: "I wish we could get an opportunity against Russia to avenge the blood of our martyrs" (Salaam Times 2022).

In short, blood revenge functions as a powerful deterrent against free-riding in irregular conflicts, heightening the costs of non-mobilisation and pushing apolitical individuals to get involved in the hostilities and avenge wrongs suffered by themselves or one of their close kinsmen. While the escalation of violence in civil war can lead to the collective mobilisation of avengers belonging to the same social group, the compelling obligation to exact blood revenge can generate a spill-over of insurgent violence, driving avengers to become foreign fighters. This "snowball" effect contributes to scale up violence in civil wars, driving scores of avengers along with their extended families into the arms of militant groups, which in turn receive constant inflows of highly motivated recruits willing to risk their lives in their quest for restoring their families' honour.

Target Selection

In traditional societies, where individuals are identified by their family or clan affiliations, guilt is rarely if ever defined in individual terms. Since the guilt of one person is cast upon his or her entire social group, avengers are traditionally entitled to exact revenge either upon the direct culprit or one of his close male kinsmen. During a civil war, the possibility to expand the pool of potential targets offers an important opportunity for avengers who either lack information on the culprit's whereabouts or the means to strike against their preferred target of choice. The principle of collective guilt, enshrined in the sociocultural custom of retaliation, allows avengers to fulfil their social obligations even when the identity of the direct culprit is unknown. In such cases, avengers may feel encouraged to direct their attacks against a wide pool of targets sharing a connection with the alleged culprit, including comrades-in-arms, members of wider military factions, as well as non-combatants sharing ethnic, religious, or cultural links with the preferred—yet unreachable—target.

Nevertheless, the loosening of the selectivity principle does not exempt avengers from attempting to strike against their preferred target. During the Second Russian–Chechen War, people would expose themselves to great risks to identify the Russian soldiers involved in sweep operations, known as *zachistka*: "if a Russian soldier was wounded while killing a family, people came to the hospital to remember his face" (Paterson 2003). Even years after the misdeed, Chechen avengers continued to hunt down Russian soldiers living outside Chechnya's borders: "Megalitres [of vodka] were spilled to get the addresses of those in charge of [sweep] operations in one village or another" (Souleimanov & Siroky 2016: 697). Similar episodes emerge from other parts of the world, as well. In July 2012, two Indonesian soldiers accidentally ran over a young boy near Wamena, a town situated in the Indonesian war-torn province of West Papua. To avenge the boy's death, the villagers stabbed to death one of the two soldiers, triggering a violent response from the entire local battalion (Webb-Gannon 2012). Similarly, in 2014, two Syrian citizens hunted down and shot dead in the Lebanese city of Amman the commander of the Liwa al-Mujahideen Brigade, a Syrian rebel militia, for his alleged involvement in the killing of the two avengers' family members (AFP 2014).

When exacting revenge on the direct culprit is unfeasible, avengers may attempt to strike against his brothers-in-arms under the assumption that they share part of the blame. In July 2000, three MEF militants walked into a hospital located in Honiara, the provincial capital of Guadalcanal, and shot dead two IFM members who allegedly took part in a gun battle the previous week with a local MEF unit (Dinnen 2000). In Chechnya, when members of locally recruited militias took part in Russian-led sweeps, avengers would consider their co-ethnics as better-suited targets because they were deemed "more guilty" than foreign troops. This was the case of a Chechen policeman who took part in a targeted abduction of an insurgent by a Russian unit in his own village. While the soldiers were probably the ones leading the operation, the toll of blood revenge was exacted on the policeman, deemed more responsible than any "outsider" (Visayeva 2006).

If none of the direct culprit's close comrades can be reached, any member belonging to the related belligerent faction may be chosen as a viable target of a blood revenge attack. As explained by a Pakistani police chief from the federally administered tribal areas of the Swat district in 2009, local villagers would avenge their relatives killed by the local branch of the Taliban movement, Tehrik-e-Taliban Pakistan (TTP), by striking against any militant that they could come across: "If they find a Talib, he will not receive any forgiveness from the people" (Khan 2009). The same logic was upheld by TTP elements after suffering casualties at the hands of the Pakistan Armed Forces. In 2012, militants belonging to a TTP unit operating in the Khyber district videotaped themselves executing 15 Pakistani soldiers in revenge for the killing of 12 of their comrades. Before shooting their captives at point blank, the militants declared:

> Twelve of our comrades were besieged and mercilessly martyred… Our pious women were also targeted. To avenge those comrades, we will kill these men. We warn the government of Pakistan that if the killing of our friends is not halted, this will be the fate of you all.
>
> (Mehsud 2012)

Interestingly, the practice of exacting blood revenge upon random members of a rival faction can often drag competing rebel groups in cycles of tit-for-tat revenge killings. In a recent article, Souleimanov and Colombo (2021) explain that the compelling obligation of avenging a fallen kinsman or comrade-in-arms is a key driving incentive behind many episodes of jihadist infighting. Once triggered, intra-rebel blood feuds can drive dozens of militants to seek vengeance for their fallen comrades, fuelling a self-reinforcing cycle of violence that grows every time a group's member is killed by a rival faction. To make an example, in July 1989, during the last year of the Soviet occupation of Afghanistan, about 30 Afghan rebels affiliated with Jamiat-i-Islami, or Islamic Society, were killed in an ambush ordered by the leader of a rival faction who was seeking revenge for the alleged killing of several of his field commanders the previous year (Coll 1989).

In other instances, both rebel and pro-government groups have instrumentalised blood revenge to justify the targeting of civilians based on their kinship, clan, or ethnic connections with members of rival factions. As recalled by a former Afghan sergeant, insurgent operatives are used to exact revenge on civilian relatives, both to satisfy their desire for retribution and to further cow their enemies into passive submission: "[Taliban fighters seeking vengeance] attacked my wife and son because I am serving in the ranks of the Afghan National Army" (Zucchino & Mangal 2019). Defined by Souleimanov et al. (2022b: 183) as "the most selective form of collective violence," the practice of targeting the relatives of rebel militants—or "kin killing"—is often upheld in conjunction with local customary practices by state-sponsored entities seeking to quell an armed insurgency. In the Egyptian province of Sinai, the regime's security forces "usually target the relatives of known insurgents" in retaliation for casualties inflicted by the militants during the successful attacks (Ashour 2019: 546). In 2014, the then-head of the North Caucasian Republic of Ingushetia, Yunus-Bek Yevkurov, stated that his government would no longer prevent soldiers from holding the insurgents' relatives as responsible for their kinsmen's misdeeds: "Until now we have acted with a great restraint and have attempted to restrain the relatives of those who were killed by the militants from taking blood revenge, but we will no longer do that" (Vatchagaev 2014).

Conceived as a form of deterrence against anti-incumbent activity, a "kin killing" policy based on the instrumentalisation of blood revenge builds upon socially sanctioned means of conflict resolution to victimise the relatives of insurgents who refuse to disengage from violence. In Chechnya, local authorities embrace the tenets of blood revenge as an official counterterrorism state policy. In a broadcast speech recorded in August 2008, Ramzan Kadyrov remarked that the relatives of insurgents were equally culpable for the deeds of their kinsmen, thus deserving the same treatment should they fail to prevent their family members from engaging in rebel activity:

[W]e must resort to Chechen customs—in the past, such people were cursed and ousted [from society]. It's normal ... those families that have relatives in the woods are all collaborators in the crime; they are terrorists, extremists, Wahhabis, and devils.

(Human Rights Watch 2009: 23)

This was the case of a Chechen woman and her family, expelled from their village in 2016 because of her brother's membership in an insurgent group: "we had three days to leave the Chechen Republic. They said that people had been killed in Grozny on ... [my brother's] orders, and now there was no place for us in Chechnya" (Sulim 2017).

In some cases, the loosening of the selectivity principle can encourage avengers to expand the pool of potential targets to entire (sub)ethnic, (sub)religious, or (sub)cultural communities, thus putting thousands of people at risk of falling victims of a blood revenge murder. Between 1988 and 1998, during the civil war erupted on the island of Bougainville, in the Solomon Islands, members of the Papua New Guinea Defence Forces (PNGDF) reportedly exacted blood revenge upon random local villagers as "payback" for the deaths of fellow servicemen at the hands of indigenous rebel groups (Amnesty International 1993: 14). Similarly, in August 2015, two Indonesian soldiers opened fire on a group of residents of Timika city, in West Papua, to exact revenge for the previous beating of one of their comrades, who disturbed a local tribal ceremony (Coalition for Enforcement of Law and Human Rights in Papua 2017: 9). For some insurgents and pro-government militants, co-ethnicity equals culpability, a form of symbolic guilt meant to channel the need to exact revenge against a whole community perceived as guilty.

Recruitment and Disengagement

Manpower is the lifeblood of rebellion and counter-rebellion. As explained by Weinstein (2006 [2007]: 99), an armed actor incapable of attracting new recruits is unlikely to pose a serious threat to the *status quo*: "Rebellion occurs only when individuals ... decide to run mortal risks by challenging the government." Nonetheless, individuals are often-times reticent to expose themselves to "mortal risks" in return for the intangible promise of collective benefits.

To encourage people to fight, armed actors typically offer "selective incentives"—economic endowments that are given out to new members as a reward for their commitment to the group. In his seminal article on the drivers of collective action amongst rural peasants, Lichbach explains that, throughout history, peasants who took part in insurgent activity often did so out of an accurate evaluation of the expected pay-offs offered by a given rebel group:

> Given that peasants have more than one potential supplier, they can comparison shop for the best deal offered by the various dissident groups and opt to join certain rural movements rather than others based on the relative selective incentives available.
>
> (Lichbach 1994: 411)

The enticement of short-term gains grants access to a readily available source of manpower to be deployed in combat operations. Nonetheless, the risk of attracting opportunistic joiners whose only interest in the group's cause are their short-term gains makes long-term retainment a highly challenging endeavour. As Weinstein (2005: 600) put it, opportunistic recruits are "ill-suited to the long-term goal of capturing state power."

In societies where the concepts of honour and retaliation endure, however, individuals may find in *non-material* incentives a far stronger motivating factor for getting recruited into an armed group. In areas where one's social status is dependent upon honour, rather than wealth, individuals will likely prioritise the defence of their families' reputation over any other form of material reward. As explained by a Congolese villager who joined a local defence militia in the 1990s against the threat posed by the *Rassemblement Congolais pour la Démocratie* (RCD), an armed group backed by Rwanda and Uganda, the compelling need to exact vengeance offset any other concern for taking part in high-risk combat operations: "I had some friends who stayed [away from the fight]. They were afraid of combat and of being killed. I did not have fear, because I wanted to avenge the death of my brother" (Richards 2014: 315).

In recruiting avengers, armed groups can swell their ranks with highly committed individuals uninterested in material rewards and unlikely to defect or free ride on their social obligations. In Afghanistan, the local population differentiated individuals who joined the Taliban out of the need to avenge a kinsmen from other recruits by using the term "*majburi*", or "forced", thus putting emphasis on the *non-material* incentives that drove apolitical tribesmen into the arms of the rebel group (Rutting 2009: 7). Across the tribal areas of Yemen, the deaths of civilians in U.S.-sponsored drone strikes pushed scores of apolitical avengers into the arms of Al-Qaeda's local branch, Al-Qaeda in the Arabian Peninsula (AQAP), which in turn deployed these recruits in high-risk combat operations against U.S.-backed military objectives (Johnsen 2013). Likewise, the Maute Group, an IS affiliate operating in the Philippines' province of

Mindanao, sought to recruit prospective avengers to be deployed during the Siege of Marawi, a five-month-long battle, which took place in 2017 between jihadi factions and security forces over the control of the provincial capital of Lanao del Sur. A former recruit recalled that the jihadists persuaded him to partake in the assault by leveraging on his desire to avenge the death of his religious leader, killed during the armed hostilities: "I got angry. I really wanted to avenge his death" (Fonbuena 2019).

Nonetheless, exacerbating blood feuds for recruitment purposes can be a double-edged sword. When an avenger who got recruited by an armed faction exacts blood revenge, the victim's kinsmen are likely to declare blood feud and seek membership in a rival group to maximise their chances of success. As the conflict drags on, more avengers are driven to join warring factions, triggering a self-enforcing recruitment cycle that breeds violence and political instability. Starting in the late 1980s, the Turkish government encouraged tribesmen from Northern Kurdistan to join the Village Guards in the fight against the PKK insurgency, promising to turn a blind eye to crimes of blood revenge. In a 1994 Turkish Parliamentary Inquiry, the commission found that new recruits took great advantage of the situation: "Several village guards have killed villagers with whom they have blood feuds based on the pretext that the latter are PKK members, and pressured these villagers to desert their villages" (Belge 2016: 299).

Although the opportunity to settle scores with impunity attracted tens of thousands of fighters, the sharp increase in intra-Kurdish feuds generated similar recruitment opportunities for the rebels. As recalled by a former full-time PKK member, the group's leadership was actively seeking to trick the security forces into launching indiscriminate military operations, which would have driven scores of avengers into the PKK's arms: "According to Apo [nickname for the then leader Abdullah Öcalan], even if 100 people were to die, still, their children would become PKK supporters [to take revenge]" (Marcus 2007: 46). Trapped into spirals of tit-for-tat revenge killings, tribesmen seeking vengeance will keep joining one armed faction or the other, thus contributing to prolonging the PKK's struggle for national independence.

In asymmetric conflicts, however, governments may exploit blood revenge to co-opt local militias and weaken the rebellion's front. During the civil war in Bougainville, the government of Papua New Guinea sponsored the establishment of the Bougainville Resistance Force (BRF), a local pro-government paramilitary force largely made up of highly motivated avengers seeking to retaliate against the Bougainville Revolutionary Army (BRA) (Bohane 2007: 155). The indigenous auxiliary force progressively replaced the PNGDF as the main pro-government actor involved in counter-insurgency operations across the island. As reported by Boege, one of the leading experts on the conflict, the presence of locally recruited pro-government militias forced the rebels to release pressure on the PNGDF and rather direct their attacks on the BRF:

> In fact, over time, it was the [Bougainville] Resistance [Force] that bore the brunt of the fighting on the government side. This changed the character of the conflict. From being a war of Bougainvilleans against 'foreign' government troops, it became a war among Bougainvilleans themselves.
>
> (Boege 2013: 10)

During the Second Russian–Chechen War of 1999–2009, the exploitation of intra-Chechen blood feuds empowered the Russians to transform a national fight for independence into a localised civil war. The co-optation of Akhmad Kadyrov, former secessionist leader and *mufti* of the separatist Chechen Republic of Ichkeria, was the first and most important step towards the indigenisation of the conflict—a policy often dubbed "Chechenisation." With his appointment to President of Chechnya in October 2003, Kadyrov along with his personal militia—known as *Kadyrovtsy*—were dragged into spiralling blood feuds with their former comrades-in-arms (Šmíd & Mareš 2015). As the war progressed, the *Kadyrovtsy* started bearing the brunt of the fighting, especially under the leadership of Ramzan Kadyrov, Akhamad's son, who took the lead of the Russian-backed Republic of Chechnya after the death of his father, killed in a bomb attack in May 2004. As a local villager explained, the establishment of a Chechen paramilitary force effectively morphed the character of the conflict, turning it from a struggle for independence into an internecine struggle: "[the Russian President Vladimir] Putin had a stroke of genius: he let Ramzan Kadyrov do the dirty work. Now it's Chechen against Chechen" (Seierstad 2008: 99).

For avengers, the risk of getting trapped in an ongoing civil war is substantial and is averted, whenever possible. This is typified in a "pact of fellowship" signed in the 1960s between the leaders of Ruhm and Subâra, two subsections of the larger Sufyân tribe, an ethnic group from Northern Yemen caught amidst the clashes between republicans and royalists. In the pact, the tribal leaders agreed that avengers who carry out a blood revenge killing should disengage from the hostilities to avert spirals of retaliatory attacks between the two communities: "If the killer is killed, that is an end of it, whether from Ruhm or /Subâra" (Dresch 2002: 11).

On many occasions, traditional authority figures continue to exercise strong influence over their communities, either giving their blessing to avengers seeking retribution or de-escalating conflicts whenever these threaten to drag entire communities into violent intra-tribal clashes. In 2016, a group of tribesmen from the Yemeni district of Hamdan ambushed a convoy of Houthi rebels seeking to avenge the deaths of two fellow villages. During the assault, the war party accidentally killed a tribesman from Hamdan, who was travelling with the rebels. Although the incident could have prompted the violent mobilisation of the victim's kinsmen, the risk was averted through the mediation of tribal elders:

> The men responsible for the killing were summoned by their tribal leaders. The tribal leader who arbitrated the case asked them to swear that they did not know that there was a member of their tribe in the truck with the Houthis when they ambushed it. The men swore under oath they did not, which under tribal terms indicated that they did not intend to kill him. By doing that, the tribe avoided the potential revenge killing this incident might have otherwise caused.
>
> (Al-Dawsari 2021: 12)

More often, however, individuals dragged into blood feuds face steep difficulties when attempting to return to civilian life. As leaving an armed group is tantamount to losing the protection benefits that come with membership, demobilised recruits expose themselves and their relatives to the risk of falling victim to retaliatory attacks. A telling example comes from the Russian-led counter-insurgency operations in Chechnya. To drain the pools of recruits for the Chechen resistance, Kadyrov started offering amnesties to former insurgents willing to come "out of the woods" and join the *Kadyrovtsy*. By forcing new recruits to openly carry out initiation killings against their former comrades-in-arms, Kadyrov dragged turncoat rebels and their families into blood feuds with their fellow countrymen, leaving them with no other option than fighting for the Russians "until the very end" (Souleimanov & Aliyev 2015: 178). As explained by a local villager whose son was kidnapped in a nightly raid, many *Kadyrovtsy* members along with their relatives may fall victim to retaliatory attacks should they be perceived as vulnerable: "Kadyrov's people are hiding behind their masks on raids like this. But if we find out who the offender is, then even a hundred years later, we will find him and take revenge" (Vayfond 2019). Similarly, members of the Kurdish pro-government militias known as Village Guards expressed concerns over the potential disbandment of their groups. One member referred that losing membership would have exposed recruits and their families to the risk of retaliatory attacks by avengers supported by the PKK: "We want peace, but we want to be safe too... What if anybody wants to take revenge on us? We have to keep our weapons to be able to defend ourselves" (Geerdink 2014).

Lastly, blood revenge can serve as a powerful counter-defection mechanism that armed groups exploit to retain fighters willing to participate in high-risk combat operations. In Somalia, the local Al-Qaeda affiliate, known as Al-Shabaab, is known to exact blood revenge against the defectors' relatives to minimise the incidence of further defections: "the father [of two defected insurgents] tried to explain that he did not know of their whereabouts, to no avail. The last time he was approached by Al-Shabaab he was killed" (LandInfo 2014: 23). This was confirmed by other human rights activists, who reported that the defectors' relatives are constantly in danger of falling victims to Al-Shabaab's revenge attacks: "If a person recruited by Al-Shabaab escapes, his brother will in turn be at potential risk by association" (NOAS 2014: 36). Given the potential repercussions, disengaging from Al-Shabaab has for long been unthinkable. As explained in 2015 by a former Al-Shabaab commander, it was only with the degradation of the insurgency's operational capabilities that defecting started becoming feasible: "There was no defection two or even one year back… The reason we have some high-value targets defecting today is because of pressure … from the Somali National Army and (the UN peacekeeping force) Amisom" (Harding 2015).

Summary

Drawing upon evidence from dozens of irregular conflicts across the globe, this chapter has provided a concise overview of the profound impact of blood revenge over key dynamics of civil wars and insurgencies, specifically the patterns of violent mobilisation, target selection, recruitment, and disengagement from violence. In cultures where concepts of honour and revenge are prominent, the obligation to eschew public humiliation compels apolitical individuals to pick up arms and exact blood revenge. As free-riding on one's moral duty is deemed as socially impermissible, avengers are incentivised to participate in high-risk combat operations *irrespective* of the mortal dangers of joining an armed group and despite a paucity of material pay-offs. Given that a wound of honour impairs the entire family, clan, or tribe, the logic of blood revenge can drive multiple kinsmen to pick up arms and seek vengeance, thus contributing to sustaining self-enforcing cycles of avengers *voluntarily* joining armed groups and facing each other on the frontlines.

Once involved in the hostilities, avengers seek to identify targets suitable for a blood revenge attack. Although the direct culprit remains the favourite target, insufficient information on his identity and whereabouts, or a lack of capabilities to strike, can motivate avengers to increase the range of viable targets which can be *rightfully* attacked. This hierarchy of targets can grow as wide as to include the direct culprit's kinsmen, his close comrades-in-arms, any member associated with the related belligerent faction, or entire (sub)ethnic, (sub)religious, or (sub)cultural groups. The inclusion of a long list of viable targets contributes to heightening the number of battle fatalities, as well as to increase the incidence of civilians killed due to their perceived ethnic, religious, or cultural ties with the direct—yet unreachable—culprit. It follows that, in conflicts occurring across areas where blood revenge is active, violence allegedly taking place under economic or ideological motives may find its true driver in locally embedded sociocultural codes.

Lastly, blood revenge offers important opportunities for recruiting fighters willing to be deployed in high-risk environments. As an avenger's chief objective is to restore his and his family's honour, the choice of mobilising into a specific armed group will likely be determined by the degree of support to be received over the quest for vengeance, rather than by short-term economic inducements offered in return for participation in life-threatening endeavours. In these contexts, armed actors assisting avengers can obtain and retain a pool of fighters unlikely to free ride on the risks associated with rebellion and counter-rebellion. In fact, for avengers, demobilisation is often impractical, as relinquishing member-ship can expose recruits and their relatives to the risk of falling victims to retaliatory attacks by avengers fighting for other warring factions. Armed groups may also weaponise blood revenge, turning it into a tool against side-switching amongst their own ranks. By deeming civilian relatives as equally liable for a recruit's misdeeds, armed actors can effectively raise the costs of non-compliance far above any prospective benefit associated with defection. In doing so, both governments and rebel factions obtain access to stable streams of highly motivated recruits unlikely to mutiny or defect. Dragged into the hostilities, avengers are compelled to keep fighting to protect their families from the threat of retaliation, thus prolonging the struggle and increasing the number of battle and civilian casualties registered in many areas where blood revenge endures.

Note

1 According to economic theory, nonrivalry indicates a condition in which the consumption of a good by an individual does not lower its availability for another consumer, whereas non-excludability indicates that no one can be excluded from consuming or enjoying the benefits associated with a particular good (Samuelson 1954). Accordingly, the typical end goal of rebel groups is

the achievement of a collective good, most commonly regime change. As argued by Collier and Hoeffel (1998: 564), "the objective of rebellion is either to capture the state or to secede from it."

References

AFP. "Jordan Says Syrian Rebel Commander Killed in Family Feud," *Alarabiya News*, July 13, 2014. Available at: https://english.alarabiya.net/News/middle-east/2014/07/13/Jordan-probes-murder-of-Syrian-rebel-commander-

Al-Dawsari, Nadwa. "Peacebuilding in the Time of War: Tribal Cease-Fire & De-escalation Mechanisms in Yemen," *Middle East Institute*, April 2021. Available at: www.mei.edu/sites/default/files/2021-04/Peacebuilding%20 in%20the%20Time%20of%20War.pdf

Amashushukeli, Mariam. "Understanding Why Youth Fight in the Middle East: The Case of Pankisi," *Center for Social Sciences*, July 2019. Available at: www.unwomen.org/sites/default/files/Headquarters/Attachments/Secti ons/Library/Publications/2019/Understanding-why-youth-fight-in-the-Middle-East-en.pdf

Amnesty International. "Papua New Guinea: 'Under the Barrel of a Gun' – Bougainville 1991 to 1993," November 19, 1993. Available at: www.amnesty. org/en/documents/asa34/005/1993/en/

Ashour, Omar. "Sinai's Insurgency: Implications of Enhanced Guerilla Warfare," *Studies in Conflict & Terrorism* 42(6), 2019: 541–558. DOI: 10.1080/ 1057610X.2017.1394653

Belge, Ceren. "Civilian Victimization and the Politics of Information in the Kurdish Conflict in Turkey," *World Politics* 68(2), April 2016: 275–306. DOI: 10.1017/s0043887115000398

Bernhart, Joslyn. "Status Competition and Territorial Aggression: Evidence from the Scramble for Africa," *Security Studies* 25(3), 2016: 385–419. DOI: 10.1080/ 09636412.2016.1195620

Bernhart, Joslyn. "The Consequences of Defeat: The Quest for Status and Morale in the Aftermath of War," *Journal of Conflict Resolution* 65(1), 2021: 195–222. DOI: 10.1177/0022002720942585

Biner, Ö. Zerrin. "Documenting 'truth' in the Margins of the Turkish State" in *Law against the State: Ethnographic Forays into Law's Transformations*, edited by Eckert, Julia; Donahoe, Brian; Strümpell, Christian & Biner, Ö. Zerrin (Cambridge: Cambridge University Press, 2012), 228–244. ISBN: 9781139043786.

Bjarnegård, Elin; Brounéus, Karen & Melander, Erik "Violent Boyhoods, Masculine Honor Ideology, and Political Violence: Survey Findings from Thailand." *Journal of Interpersonal Violence* 36(15–16), 2019: 7136–7160. DOI: 10.1177/0886260519832926.

Boege, Volker. "Bougainville Report," *The University of Queensland*, January 2013. Available at: https://espace.library.uq.edu.au/view/UQ:324976.

Bohane, Ben. "Blackfella Armies-Kastom and Conflict in Contemporary Melanesia 1994–2007," MA Thesis, University of Wollongong, 2007. Available at: https://ro.uow.edu.au/theses/648/

Brown, P. Ryan; Osterman, L. Lindsey & Barnes, D. Collin. "School Violence and the Culture of Honor," *Psychological Science* 20(11), 2009: 1400–1405. https://doi.org/10.1111/j.1467-9280.2009.02456.x

Cao, Yiming; Enke, Benjamin; Falk, Armin; Giuliano, Paola & Nunn, Nathan. "Herding, Warfare and A Culture of Honor: Global Evidence," *National Bureau of Economic Research*, Working Paper No. 29250, September 2021. DOI: 10.3386/w29250

Coalition for Enforcement of Law and Human Rights in Papua. "The Human Rights Situation in Papua," April 2017. Available at: www.upr-info.org/sites/default/files/documents/2017-04/js8_upr27_idn_e_main.pdf

Coll, Steven. "30 Killed in Afghan Rebel Feud," *Washington Post*, July 18, 1989. Available at: www.washingtonpost.com/archive/politics/1989/07/18/30-kil led-in-afghan-rebel-feud/27e77570-2d30-4862-abd1-9406d330b57f/

Collier, Paul & Hoeffler, Anke. "On Economic Causes of Civil War," *Oxford Economic Papers* 50(4), 1998: 563–573. www.jstor.org/stable/3488674

Conciliation Resources. "Women's Voices in the Bangsamoro: Experiences and Expectations in Conflict and Peace," March 2016. Available at: https://rc-servi ces-assets.s3.eu-west-1.amazonaws.com/s3fs-public/Womens%20voices%20 Bangsamoro%20WEB.pdf

Dafoe, Allan & Caughey, Devin. "Honor and War: Southern US Presidents and the Effects of Concern for Reputation," *World Politics* 68(2), 2016: 341–381. DOI: 10.1017/S0043887115000416

Dinnen, Richard. "Murder and Revenge Threaten Peace in the Solomons," *ABC News*, July 11, 2000. Available at: www.abc.net.au/am/stories/s150432.htm

Dresch, Paul. "A Pact of Brotherhood from Sufyân (Northern Yemen)," *International Journal of Archaeology and Social Sciences in the Arabian Peninsula* 10, 2002. https://doi.org/10.4000/cy.134

Findlay, Trevor. *The Use of Force in Peace Operations* (Oxford: Oxford University Press, 2002). ISBN: 0-19-829282-1.

Fonbuena, Carmela. "'They Fooled Us': The Men Who Left ISIS in the Philippines," *The Guardian*, March 9, 2019. Available at: www.theguardian. com/world/2019/mar/09/they-fooled-us-the-men-who-left-isis-in-the-philippines

Geerdink, Frederike. "Kurds Who Became 'Village Guards' and Fought PKK Rebels in Turkey to Be Disbanded – But They Fear a Betrayal," *Independent*, February 16, 2014. Available at: www.independent.co.uk/news/world/eur ope/kurds-who-became-village-guards-and-fought-pkk-rebels-in-turkey-to-be-disbanded-but-they-fear-a-betrayal-9131095.html

Gould, V. Roger. "Collective Violence and Group Solidarity: Evidence from a Feuding Society," *American Sociological Review* 64(3), June 1999: 356–380. https://doi.org/10.2307/2657491

Harding, Andrew. "Somali Defector: Why I Left al-Shabaab," *BBC News*, May 20, 2015. Available at: www.bbc.com/news/world-africa-32791713

Harkavy, E. Robert. "Defeat, National Humiliation, and the Revenge Motif in International Politics," *International Relations* 37, September 2000: 345–368. https://doi.org/10.1057/palgrave.ip.8890515

Harun al-Aswad. "Russia-Ukraine War: Syrian Rebels Seek Passage to Europe for Revenge against Putin," *Middle East Eye*, March 1, 2022. Available at: www.middleeasteye.net/news/russia-ukraine-war-syria-rebels-revenge-seek-passage

Hinton, L. Alexander. "A Head for an Eye: Revenge in the Cambodian Genocide," *American Ethnologist*, 25(3), 1998: 352–377. www.jstor.org/stable/645789

Human Rights Watch. "Easy Prey: Child Soldiers in Liberia," September 8, 1994. Available at: www.justice.gov/sites/default/files/eoir/legacy/2013/06/14/liberia_0994.pdf

Human Rights Watch. ""What Your Children Do Will Touch Upon You": Punitive House-Burning in Chechnya," July 2009. Available at: www.hrw.org/report/2009/07/02/what-your-children-do-will-touch-upon-you/punitive-house- burning-chechnya

International Crisis Group. "Lebanon's Politics: The Sunni Community and Hariri's Future Current," Middle East Report 96, May 26, 2010. Available at: www.files.ethz.ch/isn/116648/96%20Lebanons%20Politics%20-%20The%20Sunni%20Community%20and%20Hariris%20Future%20Current.pdf

International Crisis Group. "The North Caucasus Insurgency and Syria: An Exported Jihad?" Europe Report 238, March 16, 2016. www.crisisgroup.org/europe-central-asia/caucasus/north-caucasus/north-caucasus-insurgency-and-syria-exported-jihad

Johnsen, D. Gregory. "How We Lost Yemen," *Foreign Policy*, August 6, 2013. Available at: https://foreignpolicy.com/2013/08/06/how-we-lost-yemen/

Kalyvas, Stathis N. & Kocher, Matthew A. "How Free Is Free Riding in Civil Wars? Violence, Insurgency, and the Collective Action Problem." *World Politics* 59(2), January 2007: 177–216. https://doi.org/10.1353/wp.2007.0023

Khan, B. Adnan. "The Dirtiest War," *Macleans*, September 24, 2009. Available at: www.macleans.ca/news/world/the-dirtiest-war/

LandInfo. *Update on Security and Protection Issues in Mogadishu and South-Central Somalia* (Copenhagen: LandInfo, 2014). Available at: www.refworld.org/pdfid/539193314.pdf

Latifi, M. Ali & Haris, Mujtaba. "Russia-Ukraine War: Meet the Afghan Refugees Fighting Moscow's Latest Invasion," *Middle East Eye*, May 2, 2022. Available at: https://www.middleeasteye.net/fr/node/250376

Lichbach, I. Mark. "What Makes Rational Peasants Revolutionary? Dilemma, Paradox, and Irony in Peasant Collective Action," *World Politics* 46(3), 1994: 383–418. www.jstor.org/stable/2950687

Löwenheim, Oded & Heimann, Gadi. "Revenge in International Politics," *Security Studies* 17(4), 2008: 685–724. DOI: 10.1080/09636410802508055

Mairbek, Vatchagaev. "Ingushetia's Yevkurov Appears to Back Blood Revenge Against Militants' Relatives," *The Jamestown Foundation, Eurasia Daily Monitor*

11(140), July 31, 2014. Available at: www.ecoi.net/en/document/1250 360.html

Marcus, Aliza. *Blood and Belief: The PKK and the Kurdish Fight for Independence* (New York: New York University Press, 2007). ISBN-13: 978-0-8147-5711-6.

McCauley, Clark. "Toward a Psychology of Humiliation in Asymmetric Conflict," *American Psychologist* 72(3), 2017: 255–265. http://dx.doi.org/10.1037/amp 0000063

Mehsud, Saud. "Taliban Video Highlights Revenge on Pakistan Military," *Thomson Reuters*, January 21, 2012. Available at: www.reuters.com/article/us-pakistan-military-video-idUSTRE80K0NT20120121

Mountain Horse, Mike. *My People, the Bloods* (Glenbow: Alberta Institute, 1979). ISBN-10: 0919224032.

Murphy, Dan. "US Troops Rile Filipino Separatists," *The Christian Science Monitor*, February 20, 2002. Available at: www.csmonitor.com/2002/0220/p06s01-woap.html

Nawata, Kengo. "A Glorious Warrior in War: Cross-Cultural Evidence of Honor Culture, Social Rewards for Warriors, and Intergroup Conflict," *Group Processes & Intergroup Relations* 23(4), 2020: 598–611. DOI: 10.1177/1368430219838615

NOAS. *Persecution and Protection in Somalia* (Oslo: NOAS, 2014). Available at: www.noas.no/wp-content/uploads/2017/07/Persecution-and-Protect ion-in-Somalia_A-Fact-Finding-Report_2014.pdf

Olson, Mancur. *The Logic of Collective Action: Public Goods and the Theory of Groups* (Cambridge: Harvard University Press, 1965 [1971]).

Özar, Šemsa; Uçarlar, Nesrin & Aytar, Osman. *From Past to Present, A Paramilitary Organization in Turkey: Village Guard System* (Istanbul: DISA Publications, 2013). ISBN: 978-605-5458-19-5.

Parley, W. Winston. "We Hold Nothing Against Turay Family." *The New Dawn*, May 3, 2021. Available at: https://thenewdawnliberia.com/we-hold-nothing-against-turay-family/

Paterson, Scott. "As Violence Drops, Iraqi Tribes Begin to Make Amends," *The Christian Science Monitor*, October 9, 2003. Available at: www.csmonitor.com/World/Middle-East/2008/1009/p01s04-wome.html

Pitt-Rivers, Julian. "Honor," January 3, 2013. Available at: http://honorhonorho nor.blogspot.com/2013/01/honor-by-julian-pitt-rivers.html

Prothero, Mitchell. "'My MMA Gym Will be Empty': Chechens Head to Ukraine to Fight Kadyrov," *Vice News*, March 2, 2022. Available at: www.vice.com/en/article/5dgjn8/chechnya-fighters-ukraine-russia-ramzan-kadyrov

Rasmussen, E. Sune. "'My Grandsons' Fight to Avenge Their Father': Child Soldiers in Afghanistan," *The Guardian*, May 25, 2016. Available at: www.theg uardian.com/global-development/2016/may/25/child-soldiers-afghanistan-grandsons-fight-to-avenge-their-father

Ratelle, Jean-François. "Jihad at Home or Leaving for Syria and Iraq: Understanding the Motivations of Dagestani Salafists," *Perspectives on Terrorism* 14(2), 2020: 57–68. www.jstor.org/stable/26910407

Richards, Joanne. "Forced, Coerced and Voluntary Recruitment into Rebel and Militia Groups in the Democratic Republic of Congo," *Journal of Modern African Studies* 52(2), 2014: 301–326. DOI: 10.1017/S0022278X14000044

Ross, H. Marc. "A Cross-Cultural Theory of Political Conflict and Violence," *Political Psychology* 7(3), 1986: 427–469. www.jstor.org/stable/3791250

Ruttig, Thomas. "The Other Side, Dimensions of the Afghan Insurgency: Causes, Actors an Approaches to 'Talks'," *Afghanistan Analysis Network*, July 2009. Available at: www.afghanistan-analysts.org/wp-content/uploads/downloads/2012/10/200907-AAN-Report-Ruttig-The-Other-Side.pdf

Saeed, Muhammad. "Pakhtun Men's Perceptions of the Conditions Promoting Domestic Violence in their Culture," PhD Thesis, University of York, March 2012. Available at: https://core.ac.uk/download/pdf/40016969.pdf

Salaam Times. "Afghan Immigrant Fights Russian Invasion Alongside Ukrainian Soldiers," April 15, 2022. Available at: https://afghanistan.asia-news.com/en_GB/articles/cnmi_st/features/2022/04/15/feature-01

Samuelson, A. Paul. "The Pure Theory of Public Expenditure," *The Review of Economics and Statistics* 36(4), 1954: 387–389. https://doi.org/10.2307/1925895

Saoud, Dalal. "Lebanon Clans, State within a State, End Deadly Feud: Vendetta: Heads of Muslim and Christian Families Put Aside Differences after Slaying, Hail 'Historical and Brotherly Ties'," *Los Angeles Times*, June 2, 1991. Available at: www.latimes.com/archives/la-xpm-1991-06-02-mn-337-story.html

Seierstad, Åsne. *The Angel of Grozny: Orphans of a Forgotten War* (New York: Basic Books, 2008). ISBN-13: 978-0-465-01122-3.

Shuster, Simon. "Why Chechens Are Fighting Chechens in Ukraine's Civil War," *Time*, May 22, 2015. Available at: https://time.com/3893066/chechens-ukraine-war/

Šmíd, Tomáš & Mareš, Miroslav. "'Kadyrovtsy': Russia's Counterinsurgency Strategy and the Wars of Paramilitary Clans," *Journal of Strategic Studies* 38(5), 2015: 650–677. DOI: 10.1080/01402390.2014.942035

Solomon Islands Government. *Confronting the Truth for a Better Solomon Islands* (Honiara: Solomon Islands Truth and Reconciliation Commission, 2012). Available at: https://truthcommissions.humanities.mcmaster.ca/wp-content/uploads/2021/02/Solomon-Islands-Truth-and-Reconciliation-Commission_TRC_Final-Report_Vol1.pdf

Souleimanov, A. Emil. "Globalizing Jihad? North Caucasians in the Syrian Civil War," *Middle East Policy* 21(3), Fall 2014: 154–162. https://doi.org/10.1111/mepo.12090

Souleimanov, A. Emil & Aliyev, Huseyn. "Blood Revenge and Violent Mobilization: Evidence from the Chechen Wars," *International Security* 40(2), 2015: 158–180. DOI: 10.1162/ISEC_a_00219

Souleimanov, Emil A. & Aliyev, Huseyn. *How Socio-Cultural Codes Shaped Violent Mobilisation and Pro-insurgent Support in the Chechen Wars* (Cham: Palgrave Macmillan, 2017). ISBN 978-3-319-52916-5.

Souleimanov, A. Emil & Colombo, Roberto. "Vendetta and Jihadist Infighting," *Middle East Policy* 28, 2021: 68–77. DOI: 10.1111/mepo.12558

Souleimanov, A. Emil & Siroky, S. David. "Random or Retributive?: Indiscriminate Violence in the Chechen Wars," *World Politics* 68(4), 2016: 677–712. DOI: 10.1017/S0043887116000101

Souleimanov, A. Emil; Siroky, S. David & Colombo, Roberto. "Blood Revenge in Civil War: Proof-of-Concept," *Security Studies*, 2022a. DOI: 10.1080/ 09636412.2023.2153731.

Souleimanov, A. Emil; Siroky, S. David & Krause, Peter. "Kin Killing: Why Governments Target Family Members in Insurgency, and When It Works," *Security Studies* 31(2), 2022b: 183–217. DOI: 10.1080/09636412. 2022.2079997

Speckhard, Anne. "Female Suicide Bombers in Iraq," *Democracy and Security* 5(1), 2009: 19–50. DOI: 10.1080/17419160902723759

Speckhard, Anne & Ahkmedova, Khapta. "Black Widows: The Chechen Female Suicide Terrorists," *Jaffe Center for Strategic Studies*, memorandum no. 84, August 2006b: 63–80. Available at: www.inss.org.il/wp-content/uploads/2017/08/ Female-Suicide-Bombers-63-80.pdf

Speckhard, Anne & Ahkmedova, Khapta. "The Making of a Martyr: Chechen Suicide Terrorism," *Studies in Conflict & Terrorism* 29(5), 2006a: 429–492. DOI: 10.1080/10576100600698550.

Stein, Rachel. *Vengeful Citizens, Violent States* (Cambridge: Cambridge University Press, 2019). ISBN: 9781108686266.

Sulim, Sasha. "Guilty by Blood: How State Officials in Russia's North Caucasus Police Provoke and Persecute the People with Ties to Armed Insurgents," *Meduza*, October 31, 2017. Available at: https://meduza.io/en/feature/2017/ 10/31/guilty-by-blood

Tschantret, Joshua. "Honor and Terrorism: Cultural Origins of the Severity of Terrorist Attacks," *Social Science Quarterly* 101(1), January 2020: 325–345. DOI: 10.1111/ssqu.12721

Vayfond. "Disappeared Without a Trace," May 19, 2019. Available at: https://vayf ond.com/en/4029/

Visayeva, Amina. "Chechnya: Living with a Vengeance," *Institute for War & Peace Reporting*. May 30, 2006. Available at: https://iwpr.net/global-voices/chech nya-living-vengeance

Watch List. "'Who Will Care for Us?' Grave Violations against Northeastern Nigeria," 2014. Available at: https://resourcecentre.savethechildren.net/ document/who-will-care-us-grave-violations-against-children-northeast ern-nigeria/

Webb-Gannon, Camellia. "Violence in West Papua: The Vulnerable Become Indonesia's Latest Target," *The Conversation*, July 2, 2012. Available at: https:// ro.uow.edu.au/cgi/viewcontent.cgi?article=5069&context=sspapers

Weinstein, M. Jeremy. *Inside Rebellion: The Politics of Insurgent Violence* (Cambridge: Cambridge University Press, 2006 [2007]). ISBN-13: 978-0-511-34864-8.

Weinstein, M. Jeremy. "Resources and the Information Problem in Rebel Recruitment," *The Journal of Conflict Resolution* 49(4), August 2005: 598–624. DOI: 10.1177/0022002705277802

Zucchino, David & Mangal, J. Farooq. "Seeking Revenge, Taliban Target Afghan Soldiers' Families," *The New York Times*, July 10, 2019. Available at: www.nyti mes.com/2019/07/10/world/asia/taliban-revenge-afghanistan.html

5   The Erosion of Blood Revenge in Irregular Warfare

When the traditions underpinning life in cultures of honour fade away, societies undergo far-reaching changes in power relations and sociocultural structures. Yet, the erosion of blood revenge falls far from constituting an irreversible process, and when the structural conditions related to its decline are compromised, the potential for a comeback in violent self-help justice is heightened.

For blood revenge to disappear, both processes of state centralisation and societal rejection of kinship-based vengeance must come to completion. As we have shown in Chapter 4, this is easier said than done: the mechanisms triggering the decline of blood revenge are extremely complex, require a considerable amount of time to bear fruits, and are unlikely to work when society experiences recurring sociopolitical instability. In this chapter, we discuss the impact of blood revenge in irregular conflicts where the custom is or was subsiding.

The Breakdown of State Authority

State collapse is arguably one of the most common causes of the resurgence of blood revenge in irregular conflicts. Lacking a security apparatus capable of enforcing law and order, societies often experience a transformative process, often dubbed "retribalisation," centred on the reinvigoration of tribal structures and traditional customs at the expense of state institutions and national identities (Bar 2020). As argued by Ronfeldt (2006: 61), the tribal form constitutes the "natural fallback option" for communities experiencing state collapse amidst a civil war—a coping mechanism made necessary by the breakdown of state institutions. In a virtually lawless environment, long-suppressed traditional customs, such as the code of retaliation, are resurrected in an attempt to maintain some sort of order and social structure at the community level. As war drags on, the violent mobilisation of avengers into the ranks of armed groups

DOI: 10.4324/9781003387527-5

shapes the dynamics of violence, often turning political struggles into internecine conflicts driven and sustained by the logic of blood revenge.

This process was perhaps nowhere more pervasive and systematic than across modern-day Iraq. In this country, the process of state centralisation initiated under the nationalist regime of the 1960s, and accelerated by the Ba'ath Party in the 1970s, was inhibiting traditional customary codes, including the practices of blood revenge and blood money, known as *fasel* or *diya* in Arabic. As explained by a former Iraqi army officer, the central government heavily criminalised these practices, going as far as passing a law in 1997 outlawing the use of *fasels* across major urban districts: "During the rule of the 'Arifs ['Abdul Salam and 'Abdul Rahman] and Saddam Husayn, *fasel* was cancelled—gone. The state was strong enough to overcome the system by threatening legal action against anyone who takes revenge on a killer" (Carroll 2011: 19).

All that changed, when the power vacuum left by the fall of the Ba'ath Party in 2003 and the country's descent into civil war gave renewed strength to a custom that was waning away in the once heavily policed urban areas (Baram 1997). With hundreds of Iraqis waiting for the propitious time to retaliate for the brutalities inflicted by Saddam's repressive regime, cycles of tit-for-tat killings rapidly escalated in a virtually lawless environment. While Coker (2003) reported that blood revenge killings were becoming "the fastest growing crime in Baghdad and in other major Iraqi cities," local Iraqis were witnessing first-hand the outcome of the unprecedented wave of retaliatory violence. "I saw four or five (revenge killings) myself last week, and I work six-hour shifts," stated a hospital employee in Sadr City, showing no surprise for the upsurge of retaliatory murders: "we're all expecting a lot of revenge" (Carnegie 2003).

It did not take long for these predictions to come true. In many cities occupied by U.S. forces, the use of lethal force to curb protests and maintain law and order was often a key enabler of revenge-driven insurgent activity. In his account of the first stages of the war, Iraqi scholar al-Assafi illustrated how the killing of an 18-year-old protester by the U.S. forces in Ramadi compelled dozens of local avengers to form an insurgent cell:

> these people whose youth was killed by the Americans, they formed a cell, and they started looking for revenge. They found out that placing an IED is a simple matter, so a lot of cells began forming all over the place.
>
> (Montgomery & McWilliams 2009: 33)

The city of Fallujah, one of the least affected by violence in the early stages of the invasion, experienced surges of insurgent activity when local tribesmen were either shot dead by the U.S. soldiers or accidentally killed in military raids. As explained by local citizens, the killing of their fellow tribesmen could not be left unavenged: "If I see an American, I will definitely kill him if I can" (Georgy 2003). This was further remarked by a local sheik, who explained how the custom of blood revenge was pushing hundreds of apolitical tribesmen into the ranks of insurgent groups: "if the Americans continue to behave like this, the whole of Iraq will be holy warriors… To us in Fallujah, the most important thing is respect" (Tampa Bay Times 2003).

The mobilisation of avengers into the ranks of the local Al-Qaeda affiliate known as Al-Qaeda in Iraq (AQI) provided the jihadi insurgency with highly motivated recruits willing to be deployed in high-risk combat operations. Nonetheless, the resurgence of the code of retaliation across the tribal areas ended up being a double-edged sword for the insurgents. In its attempt to maintain control over the governorate of Al-Anbar, AQI engaged in a systematic campaign of intimidation against the local population, killing tribesmen either serving within the Iraqi security forces or showing defiance towards the jihadists (Kagan 2007: 6–7). Recalling his time as a serviceman in Ramadi, a U.S. soldier told the story of how, in a gun battle, the cousin of an Anbari sheik serving within the border police neutralised two AQI elements before being himself killed in the firefight. When, during his funeral, AQI militants killed in retaliation two other tribesmen, the entire tribe rose alongside its leader in a full-blown blood feud with the jihadists (Malkasian 2017: 119).

The cycle of tit-for-tat revenge killings between AQI and local tribesmen was exacerbated during the Sunni tribes' open revolt against Al-Qaeda in mid-2007 (Phillips 2009). Appalled by AQI's methods, the population started considering the jihadis as targets of blood revenge attacks. As remarked by a tribal leader: "We began to see what they [AQI] were actually doing in Anbar province. They were not respecting us or honoring us in any way … their tactics were not acceptable" (Fletcher 2006). With the tribes turning against the insurgents, AQI's deployment of blood revenge backfired. Innes (2012: 66) reports a case of a sheik who approached the Coalition forces after that AQI killed ten of his relatives in vengeance. Other locals wishing to avenge the deaths of their relatives even mobilised into the ranks of a militia known as "Anbar Revenge Brigade," specifically created for hunting down and exacting blood revenge on AQI elements. After killing five top-ranked AQI members, the group posted on its online website an announcement to testify its accomplished revenge: "Your brothers, heroes of the Revenge Brigade, carried out the killing of five important elements of al-Qaeda group, avenging the death of the sons of our Ramadi city" (Khalil 2006). With the jihadists expelled from Anbar, the reckoning for the brutalities inflicted on the population was redirected against the families whose sons joined the insurgency: "all of the pain lands on them,' explained a local tribal leader, because 'people want their revenge. They'll storm the house and kill everyone there. They just want to be satisfied" (Healy & Al-Jawoshy 2011).

A similar process characterised the resurgence of blood revenge killings across the islands situated in the North Solomons Province of Papua New Guinea (PNG). In the 1970s, the central government initiated a process aimed at suppressing the customary practice of "payback" killings through the institutionalisation of monetary forms of compensation, locally known as "blut moni" (blood money). The introduction of the principle of blood money during legal processes was met with enthusiasm by international observers, who stressed that the practice would have likely had "a dramatic deterrent effect on payback killings and crimes in rural areas generally" (Barnett 1972 cited in Gordon 1981: 97). Nevertheless, the government's inability to tackle corruption and enforce law and order contributed to driving people away from institutionalised forms of justice and towards traditional forms of conflict settlement—including blood revenge. As reported by Gordon (1981: 100), the lack of trust in judicial institutions was pushing people to take matters in their own hands: "The most obvious indicator of the government's loss of authority is the recent upsurge in payback killings of people while in official custody."

The upsurge in homicides motivated by blood revenge played a major role during the civil war in Bougainville, which lasted ten years and claimed the lives of about 15,000 people (United Nations 2005). Clashes erupted in late 1988, when local clansmen seized control over the Australian-operated Panguna mine and established a militia force, known as the Bougainville Revolutionary Army (BRA), in response to the deployment of contingents of the Papua New guinea Defence Forces (PNGDF). The presence of "foreign" troops engaged in counter-insurgency operations on the island contributed to swelling the ranks of the BRA with volunteers seeking to avenge their kinsmen killed during the hostilities. As reported by a former child soldier, the desire for "payback" was a strong motivating factor for joining the local militias:

> Why do I feel angry, why did I join the BRA to fight? They [PNGF forces] killed my brother and uncle (an old man) when they went [to the fields] … We want[ed] to go and make payback with them, remove them from our area. I discussed [joining the BRA] with my parents. They tried to stop me, but I was too determined… They were worried about me staying there and finally said, okay, I can go.
> (Emmons 2002: 28)

Nonetheless, for many locals, joining the BRA offered unprecedented opportunities for settling scores with their fellow islanders. In a report documenting the human rights violations in Bougainville during the first years of the conflict, Amnesty International (1990: 38) referred that several BRA attacks against unarmed civilians were carried out as part of "payback" assaults motivated by the logic of blood revenge—a phenomenon that only grew in intensity as the conflict progressed. Largely in response to the BRA's brutalities, scores of Bougainvilleans decided to join the Bougainville Resistance Force (BRF), a pro-government indigenous militia whose ranks were filled with avengers seeking violent redress.

The mobilisation of avengers into the arms of local paramilitary units added a layer of apolitical grievances atop a struggle for national independence, triggering cycles of tit-for-tat revenge killings involving both fighters and innocent civilians. As confirmed by a study sponsored by the U.S. government, the involvement of locally recruited fighters contributed to "indigenise" the conflict, now fought predominantly amongst Bougainvilleans: "Though ostensibly fighting for the BRA or the BRF, local groups engaged in private wars to avenge personal or social-kin group grievances or settle old land disputes" (Ipp & Cooper 2013: 6).

The hostilities between the two groups started drawing to a close in 1997, when peace talks between the warring parties culminated in the signing of a peace agreement and the creation of an Autonomous Bougainville Government in June 2005. Nonetheless, the demobilisation and disarmament programme to which the BRA leadership had agreed upon failed to put a halt to the cycles of revenge killings, which dragged on long after the formal end to the hostilities. As reported by Amnesty International in 1997, many former BRA members became targets of "payback" attacks at the end of the conflict:

> Despite surrendering, former BRA members are vulnerable to revenge attacks by the Resistance Forces and the PNGDF, not least because members of the PNGDF, few of whom are Bougainvillean, often feel vulnerable… Of the unlawful killings and "disappearances" recorded by Amnesty International since 1993, at least 13 individuals are believed to have been killed or "disappeared" after having been arrested by the PNGDF either in or on leaving Care Centres, usually on suspicion of involvement with the BRA.
>
> (Amnesty International 1997: 24)

In many cases, these cycles of tit-for-tat killings were driven and exacerbated by the actions of female non-combatants, who encouraged their male kinsmen to join local armed groups and exact revenge upon members of rival factions. In 2007, scores of avengers from the Oria community mobilised into a local militia group, known as the Wisai Liberation Movement (WILMO), to carry out retaliatory attacks against other ethnic groups deemed responsible for crimes that occurred during the Bougainville Civil War of 1989–1999. As reported by a local female villager, women played an important role in pushing their husbands and sons to seek vengeance:

> Yes, we don't carry the guns and fight, but we tell our sons and the men in our community to hate and to take up arms. We knew that we had influenced the men here to hate our brothers outside, to go and kill when someone is killed from our community.
>
> (Holmberg 2016)

Nonetheless, the potential for a new resurgence of payback killings in Bougainville has been partially offset by the widespread availability of traditional conflict resolution mechanisms. Ever since the end of the hostilities, hundreds of Bougainvilleans decided to reconcile and officially renounce their claims of blood revenge. As explained by a former BRA commander, people who take part in traditional rituals of forgiveness are exempt from suffering the social sanctions otherwise imposed on failed avengers:

> When we reconcile I am the first person to say: "I caused the problem, I have done this and I am sorry." The other person then says: "I accept your apology and I forgive you. I won't take revenge on you." During the ceremony we would sign a piece of paper saying we are now reconciled.
>
> (Reddy 2008: 125)

When avengers reconcile, they renounce all claims of revenge against the culprit and his kinsmen. As explained by Joseph Canisius Kabui, former BRA commander and first president of the Autonomous Region of Bougainville, an avenger who spoils the peace after reconciling is to be killed by his kinsmen and fellow tribesmen: "The moment the hatchet is buried, it stays buried. Anyone seen to be digging up the buried hatchet will get the most severe punishment. This means death" (Braithwaite et al. 2010: 73).

The resurgence of payback killings during the Bougainville Civil War, and its impact over the dynamics of insurgency and counter-insurgency warfare, closely resembles the patterns of violence registered in the

Egyptian province of Sinai. In 2011, the toppling of President Hosni Mubarak and the country's subsequent descent into political instability allowed militant groups affiliated with Al-Qaeda and the Islamic State (IS) to take root in the rural areas of Upper Egypt, where the security forces were no longer capable of enforcing law and order. The departure of military contingents from Sinai contributed to giving new impetus to long-simmering blood feuds, which had experienced a slow decline since the 1990s (Maslouh 2018: 4). As explained by a local tribesman from al-Kosheh, a village in Upper Egypt, a blood feud can remain lenient for a long time before resurfacing at times of political instability:

> It doesn't stop until someone in one of the families wants to stop and agrees to go through a ceremony to officially halt the killings. This is the only thing that can stop it. Other than that, it will never stop at all.
>
> (Nazir 2016)

To suppress the growing insurgency, locally recruited security forces resorted to a policy of collective responsibility, threatening to exact revenge upon the rebels' families to force the insurgents into capitulation. Nevertheless, for many villagers, the brutalities inflicted on their fellow kinsmen could not be left unanswered. As reported by a local tribesman, dozens of avengers were ready to mobilise into local militias and defend their clan and families' honour:

> They [the police] will take revenge, but don't worry, we are alert… If the police came here tomorrow and killed all the men, the next day, there would be triple the number of men… We are insulted in our country. Insulted. This is unacceptable. It is unacceptable to be insulted in my house.
>
> (Giglio & Dickey 2013)

While the government might have compelled numerous insurgents into demobilisation, its aggressive measures antagonised hundreds of local villagers who were craving revenge. As explained by a local observer, many young people have been "politicised by violence, by seeing friends or family members shot and killed by police … [and] now want vengeance" (Rohan 2015).

The violent mobilisation of avengers was also exploited by local actors seeking to attract highly motivated recruits willing to be deployed in high-risk combat operations. In 2013, the jihadi group known as Ajnad Misr launched an anti-police campaign labelled "Retribution is

Life" specifically aimed at recruiting tribesmen wishing to avenge the deaths of their kinsmen killed by the Egyptian security forces (Awad 2014). Similarly, tribes who suffered casualties at the hands of the militants encouraged their members to join pro-government forces and exact revenge. Following a major terrorist attack by IS militants on November 24, 2017, the leaders of the Sawarka tribe of Northern Sinai issued a statement prompting their fellow tribesmen to avenge their relatives: "For all who want revenge and punishment of this black terror and take revenge on IS and those who committed the crime of today and yesterday, we, again, welcome everyone to join the tribal fighters" (Shalabi 2017).

Although the current government, under the leadership of Abdel Fattah el-Sisi, has been increasing efforts aimed at solving outstanding blood feuds through the assistance of tribal elders, the ongoing hostilities are likely to keep driving avengers into the arms of militant groups, indefinitely prolonging cycles of tit-for-tat revenge killings (Galal 2019). As anticipated by a local villager in 2013, the risk of blood feuds escalating and spiralling out of control threatens to drag the conflict on in Sinai for many years to come:

> Nobody can control Upper Egypt vengeance. And now everybody has guns... I am not saying that it will be [a] civil war. But at least Upper Egypt will go back to the '70s or '80s, [when] people were shooting at police officers just because they were police officers.
>
> (Giglio & Dickey 2013)

The Transition to a Culture of Retaliation

For societies in which blood revenge has largely subsided under the combined effects of state centralisation and societal modernisation, the occurrence of civil war can consolidate lingering cultural predispositions to violence, typically enshrined in concepts of male honour and warrior ethos. Although blood revenge may no longer survive as an institutionalised customary code, its remnants continue to underpin socially sanctioned forms of retaliatory violence driven by the belief that men ought to safeguard their honour against affronts or perceived injustices (Nisbett & Cohen 1996). No longer guided by the tightly codified principles of blood revenge, individuals are largely left free to decide if, when, and why a perceived wrong or insult is worthy of a retaliatory response. Accordingly, episodes that can drive avengers to violent mobilisation multiply in scope and character, becoming much more "personal" and dependent upon the individual's own perception of what constitutes a wound of honour. We define this societal condition as a "culture of retaliation," differentiating it from the more structured set of norms underpinning the endurance of customary codes, such as blood revenge.

The presence of the culture of retaliation was particularly noticeable in Syria, a country where public reforms and rapid urban growth in the 1960s sparked a progressive erosion of customary laws, including blood revenge (Elkabir 1983). When, in March 2011, clashes between protestors and security forces degenerated in civil war, countless individuals who suffered humiliation sought to become avengers and retaliate against the perceived culprits. As reported by a civil right activist from Homs, the presence of only a handful of avengers was enough to initiate escalating cycles of tit-for-tat killings between different neighbourhoods: "Maybe most just stay home and mourn. But all it takes is for one person to go and say, 'I want revenge'. So suddenly you get these cases where some people are taken are killed" (Hamilton & Solomon 2011). No longer part of ritualised forms of compensatory justice, revenge killings remained largely unregulated, with their execution and modality left to the avenger's own volition. In 2012, for instance, a Syrian rebel taped himself dismembering a Syrian soldier and eating his organs in revenge for the victim's alleged humiliation of a woman and her two daughters. Confronted with international outrage, the rebel justified his actions as a rightful response to a perceived humiliation, in accordance with his own interpretation of local practices of violent retaliation: "Our slogan is an eye for an eye and a tooth for a tooth" (AFP 2013a).

The incidence of blood revenge killings was exacerbated by the dissolution of the selectivity principles underpinning traditional forms of blood revenge. In societies where customary codes have eroded, tribal affiliations and kinship loyalties tend to break, leading to the atomisation of the families of tribesmen turned into urbanised town-dwellers (Reader 1970). The change in the structural composition of nuclear families, in turn, drives a shift in traditional cultural practices, including publicly sanctioned means of individual retaliation. Although holding close family members as collectively culpable because they share the same *blood* ceases being conceived as a socially acceptable practice, the range of potential culprits may be substantially enlarged according to the avenger's own perception of what constitutes guilt. Rather than seeking to exact revenge upon the individual who is most responsible for an injustice, avengers may arbitrarily attack anyone perceived to be part of the "guilty" group. As reported by a Syrian clansman in 2011, avengers are largely left free to decide whether to take revenge against the direct culprit or rather attack any member of his community: "If one of the tribe is shot by a member of the security services and the killer is not properly punished by the government, then another security man will be killed to settle the score. It's simple: an eye-for-an-eye" (Sands 2011).

In areas where the culture of retaliation runs strong, avengers might be driven to violence by a combination of personal *and* ideological motives. In contrast to institutionalised forms of blood revenge, which triggers are exquisitely apolitical, avengers from areas where customary codes have eroded may find in political grievances a viable reason for seeking violent redress. This was the case of dozens of former rebels affiliated with the Free Syrian Army (FSA), who joined a pro-government unit to exact revenge upon militants of the local IS affiliate, known as Jaysh Khalid bin al-Waleed (JKBW), for both personal and ideological reasons:

> I can recognise many of them [JKBW members] and I know their clans very well, I will follow them to the end of the earth, and we will take our revenge on them for degrading, killing and slaughtering our people [Daraa] ... I do not care under whose command I fight Daesh, Russian or Syrian, I just wanted to take revenge for the blood of my relatives *and* for the wasted revolution.
>
> (Al-Jabassini 2019: 18, emphasis added)

As the war dragged on, the lack of conflict resolution mechanisms contributed to bringing concepts of honour and revenge to the fore of social life. Interviewed by a team of international researchers in 2016, a resident of Aleppo, Syria's second largest city, explained how the desire to seek vengeance compelled hundreds of young Syrians to participate in the armed hostilities, scaling up the conflict's death toll: "over 90% of Syrian youth seek revenge due to the death of their family members and this is what prompts them to join [in the] violence" (Aubrey et al. 2016: 11).

These considerations resonate with the justifications provided by many young men who took up arms throughout the conflict. For a 16-year-old teenager from Tlaleen, a city in the province of Aleppo, joining the ranks of the FSA offered an opportunity to avenge his father, an FSA fighter who was killed in the hostilities: "I want to avenge the death of my father" (AFP 2013b). In the same vein, a 22-year-old tribesman from the city of Baghouz joined the Kurdish-led militia known as Syrian Democratic Forces (SDF) to retaliate against IS elements for the deaths of his relatives: "I want to avenge my brother and my relatives. I will fight to the bitter end of the battle, and then I'll hunt down their sleeper cells" (El-Husseini 2019). In both cases, avengers did not bother finding out the direct culprit; any member of the "guilty" community is to be considered a viable and legitimate target of a revenge attack performed to restore an individual's wounded honour. The consolidation of the culture of retaliation in Syria emerges, for instance, in the comments of a schoolboy, who explained that his desire for vengeance blazed stronger than any other prospect that the school system could offer for his adult life:

> I still have six years of study to get my high school degree, then I need five years to graduate from college. I don't want that. I want to kill the person who killed my father because I might die in one of the bombings one day. I want to hold arms, and I want to avenge my father and all the other martyrs.
>
> (ICTJ 2018: 70)

The diffusion of the culture of honour was even acknowledged by Syrian authorities, who reportedly supported the reintegration of an 18th-century legislation known as "Blood Spill" in the province of Swaida, allowing the reintroduction of customary practices in an attempt to empower local tribal leaders (Ezzi 2017). In Syria, the outbreak of civil war gave new impetus to retaliatory practices inspired by remnants of old sociocultural customs, which have now returned in full swing across many war-torn regions of the country. As avengers may decide to act years after the triggering episode, cycles of tit-for-tat revenge might spiral out of control, thus prolonging the collective trauma of civil war.

Equally concerning was the consolidation of a culture of retaliation in Dagestan, a republic situated in Russia's North Caucasus Federal District, where the spill-over of insurgent activity from the neighbouring Chechnya engulfed the region in a protracted low-level conflict. Under firm control of the Soviet state since the 1920s, Dagestan underwent a sustained modernisation process, which progressively eroded the role of clan identities and customary laws, including blood revenge. Accordingly, information retrieved from reports of the Ministry of Internal Affairs of Dagestan shows that episodes of blood feuds dropped from 118 in 1929 to 22 in 1931, down to only 4 in 2007, thus signalling a growing rejection of kin killing practices as a socially acceptable form of conflict resolution mechanism (Musaeva 2015). Nonetheless, the fall of the Soviet Union, and the subsequent deterioration of local state institutions, contributed to bringing back remnants of age-old archaic customs, such as blood revenge. As Reynolds put it,

> the breakdown of the economy, the near collapse of the Russian state, and the ensuing struggle for resources in the 1990s reinvigorated the

role of clan and ethnic ties. Indeed, the need for protection from and the desire for revenge against poorly trained, corrupt, and occasionally sadistic police breathed new life into institutions like vendetta.

(Reynolds 2013: 6)

In fact, armed clashes between jihadist insurgents and local law enforcement agencies accelerated the comeback of retaliatory practices inspired by traditional concepts of honour and revenge. Drawing upon evidence collected during interviews with (former) Dagestani insurgents and their relatives, Ratelle and Souleimanov (2017) found that most Dagestani insurgent recruits joined the fray to either take revenge for a personal humiliation or retaliate against the local authorities for their lack of respect for local customs and traditions. In September 2015, for instance, five huntsmen who collaborated with Dagestani security forces were gunned down in a forest in southern Dagestan, allegedly by members of a local insurgent cell which was targeted by law enforcement agencies (The Moscow Times 2015). Adhering to collectively endorsed social concepts of honour and revenge, some Dagestani women even volunteered to serve as suicide bombers in the ranks of jihadi groups to avenge the death of a brother, father, or husband (Schepp 2010).

For Dagestani jihadi groups, the lingering presence of a culture of retaliation was a boon for recruiting and retaining a pool of highly motivated volunteers. Enraged and humiliated by the abuses of the local authority forces, countless locals sought membership in local armed groups for revenge, only to then be progressively radicalised and introduced to the "path of jihad." As expounded in a report by International Crisis Group (2008: 13), the desire for revenge—rather than any affinity with radical ideologies—was the primary driver for insurgent recruitment in the region: "first-hand experience of police brutality and corruption feeds a desire for revenge amplified by Islamist video propaganda inciting people to join the 'resistance movement'." Once recruited into a jihadi group, avengers frequently came to impute social decadence, corruption, abuses, and spoiled traditions to the perceived incompetence of local authorities, who then became the preferred targets of retributive attacks. As explained by Souleimanov and Aliyev, the ideological indoctrination received by new recruits prompted many avengers to consider anyone wearing police uniforms or military patches as ideal targets of repeated retaliatory attacks:

Sometimes, this extension of the enemy image propelled avengers into a vicious cycle of violence, with avengers adopting a "lone wolf" strategy, and carrying out multiple attacks on members of law enforcement agencies, which would extend over months, sometimes even years.

(Souleimanov & Aliyev 2014: 73)

The increase in the numbers of civilians and security officials killed in clashes with rebel formations motivated, in turn, dozens of avengers to join local police units or pro-government paramilitary groups. In 2012, a group of Dagestani vigilantes calling themselves "Robin Hoods" released a video claiming that they were taking up arms against the rebels out of the desire to avenge friends and relatives killed whilst serving in local police units (Vatchagaev 2012). As explained by a police lieutenant from Makhachkala, Dagestan's provincial capital, the penchant for revenge is strong amongst police officers who lost their kinsmen or comrades-in-arms during clashes with the insurgents: "If my colleague is shot before my eyes, of course something burns in me, I want revenge. That's how war works. It's a crooked balance sheet" (de Carbonnel 2012). As it is with the recruits of jihadi groups, avengers mobilised in pro-government militias often see anyone who is a Salafist as a symbolic target for a retaliatory attack. Over the years, several human rights organisations thoroughly documented the harassment and abuses inflicted by law enforcement offices on Dagestani Salafis out of alleged connections with the rebels "from the woods." As recalled by a resident, members of police units would often assume that a civilian Salafi would be somehow associated with the jihadi insurgency, and could thus become a passable target for a retaliatory attack:

> On one occasion, an officer kept pressing me, "So, how come you aren't in the woods yet? A few of your relations have been there for a while, what's stopping you? Why won't you join them?" It feels like they're actually trying to push me out, make me run for the forest.
>
> (Human Rights Watch 2015: 45)

Although the Dagestani authorities largely succeeded in containing the rebellion, the systematic targeting of individuals deemed as potentially involved in the insurgency has generated widespread resentment, and desire for revenge, amongst the population. As explained by Fueller, an expert on Caucasian politics, the cycle of tit-for-tat revenge killings in Dagestan has grown out of proportion as the conflict progressed, pushing countless militants along with their families to seek opportunities for "settling scores" and taking part in acts of *blood-taking*:

> over the years the militants have targeted almost exclusively the police and the police have retaliated by targeting not just the militants but

anyone who is Salafi, even if they are absolutely peaceful. And this, of course, has become a vicious circle.

(cited in Recknagel 2012)

In other cases, insurgent groups operating in areas where customary codes have largely eroded may embrace the culture of retaliation to showcase toughness and enhance group cohesion. In the Mediterranean island of Corsica, the separatist terrorist group known as the National Liberation Front of Corsica (FLNC) systematically upheld the local customary law of "vendetta" whenever one of its militants was killed by either the French authorities or some other rival group. When, in August 2001, François Santoni, one of the group's key leaders, was killed by former associates who he accused of having struck a deal with local organised criminal gangs, the armed wing of the FLNC promptly declared "vendetta" upon the culprits: "The assassination of our brother François Santoni will not remain unpunished for long" (Jeffries 2001). The FLNC's practice of avenging fallen militants contributed to the revival of a fading custom, which now runs largely unregulated and unchecked. As explained by a local resident: "In this way, the cycle of 'vendetta' is perpetuated, a 'vendetta' which was in the past so rigorously codified…Killing to repair [a wrong], an infernal spiral [of revenge]" (Albertini 2017: 53).

For the Maoist-inspired insurgency of the Naxalites, a left-wing guerrilla group operating in Central and East India, embracing the culture of retaliation grants access to a potent deterrent against prospective side-switchers. In January 2020, a group of Naxalites operating in the district of Dantewada, in the state of Chhattisgarh, killed the younger brother of a turncoat rebel, who defected a year earlier and joined a police unit. According to local sources, the rebels retaliated against the brother to punish the deserter for his alleged role in the killing of a senior Maoist by law enforcement officers, which occurred in April 2019 (Verma 2020). Similarly, in July 2019, the cadres of a Naxalite unit operating in the tribal areas of the district of Visakhapatnam, in the state of Andhra Pradesh, executed two local villagers in revenge for their alleged role in the killing of a rebel leader in October 2014 (Bhattacharjee 2019). In unearthing the remnants of a largely eroded customary code, the insurgents lowered the risk of defiance by signalling that acts of non-compliance will be conceived as humiliations calling for a swift retaliatory response.

Although contemporary retaliatory practices might have departed from the highly institutionalised configuration of blood revenge, their presence continues to shape the inception, course, and aftermath of civil wars and insurgencies, and thus bear important implications for the conduct of irregular warfare and counter-insurgency operations.

Takeaways for Irregular Warfare Professionals

Ranging from the North Caucasian regions of Chechnya and Dagestan to the Middle Eastern battlegrounds of Syria and Iraq, from the war-torn areas of Afghanistan and Pakistan in Central Asia to the remote islands of PNG and the Solomon Islands, down to the contested districts of Central India as well as the terrorism-hit territories of Corsica, Kosovo, and the Philippines, the evidence presented in this book points to one major consideration: sociocultural intelligence in irregular conflicts matters. As remarked by a U.S. military fusion cell officer, failing to appreciate the importance of local sociocultural codes can endanger the success of a military operation from its very outset: "In the early days of [the wars in] Afghanistan and Iraq, our inability to understand that their respective military cultures are dramatically different than ours created a myriad of problems" (Bradshaw & Esser 2018: 2).

In advocating for the important role of sociocultural intelligence in irregular conflicts, this book offered a thorough cross-case analysis of blood revenge, a key sociocultural code that irregular warfare professionals are very likely to encounter over the course of their deployments in foreign theatres of operations. Although traditional, institutionalised versions of this age-old custom have largely been eroded by the combined processes of state centralisation and societal modernisation, retaliatory practices inspired by the remnants of blood revenge remain widely diffused and can flare up in civil wars and insurgencies. Running largely unregulated and unchecked, these "eroded" retributive practices grant avengers large freedom of choice in deciding what constitutes a "wound of honour," which modality of attack is most appropriate, and who can be considered a legitimate target for a revenge attack. At times of war, this "culture of retaliation" drives scores of avengers into the ranks of armed militias, who then contribute to heightening the numbers of individuals targeted due to an alleged connection with the individuals or groups of individuals deemed as guilty of a particular offence. Drawing upon the evidence presented in this and other chapters, the present section provides a list of takeaways for irregular warfare professionals planning and executing military operations in countries where sociocultural codes linger.

While arguing that enhanced sociocultural intelligence can assist practitioners in improving their operational blueprints, we nevertheless advise our readers against considering socio-anthropological knowledge as a "silver bullet solution" in counter-insurgency and stability operations. As former NATO counter-propaganda adviser in Afghanistan and trained anthropologist Alexei Gavriel (2014: 20) put it, sociocultural intelligence is neither the magical "uncovering of a hidden or secret code of a foreign society, [nor the guarantee] that the mastering of this code allows unrestricted control over a population." In other words, sociocultural intelligence provides specialised insights from experts of anthropology, ethnology, sociology, among other disciplines, who are well-positioned to advise practitioners on how locally embedded cultural practices shape the operational environment, drive the behaviour of indigenous populations, and impact the decision-making process of both adversaries and local partners.

Takeaway no. 1: Ignore Sociocultural Intelligence at Your Own Peril

For countless individuals living in societies with strong concepts of honour and revenge, the decision to participate in armed conflicts finds its motivation in deeply embedded sociocultural norms of conduct, rather than in economic incentives or ideological affinities with extremist groups. Lack of cultural sensitivity, disinterest in understanding local power structures, failure to comply with local customary codes, and a pre-disposition to insult the locals' honour are far more common triggers of pro-insurgent violent mobilisation than any effort by insurgent actors to attract recruits through ideological narratives or economic inducements.

According to diplomats and soldiers deployed in Iraq and Afghanistan, it was the Coalition's failure to appreciate the cultural aspects of the tribal society that drove local citizens into the arms of insurgent groups. When, in November 2003, Marco Calamai, former special counsellor of the Coalition Provisional Authority (CPA) in Iraq's southern province of Dhi Qar, resigned from his position, he explained how the Coalition's lack of cultural awareness was creating "delusion, social discontent, and anger" amongst many Iraqis, thus allowing jihadi groups to "easily take root" across the country (Associated Press 2003). Similarly, a former British soldier who served in Afghanistan explained that most of the Afghan soldiers who attacked fellow Western servicemen did so out of the desire to seek vengeance for a perceived insult, rather than for any ideological affiliation with the Taliban:

> The genesis, or [source] of resentment, that seems to have fed into moments when Afghan soldiers have turned their weapons [on Western soldiers] seems to be because they perceive themselves being slighted by being shouted at, or some sort of perceived insult... Very few of these attacks seem to be about somebody who has a political, religious, or ideological hatred of Westerners in Afghanistan or who is an out-and-out Taliban sympathiser.

(Bezham 2012)

In all these cases, leveraging cultural expertise to address sociocultural drivers of violence can offer practitioners important opportunities for preventing violent extremism and stemming the tide of locals joining insurgent groups out of vengeance. In Afghanistan, the U.S.-led coalition sponsored in 2012 the distribution of a "Brochure for Understanding the Culture of Coalition Forces," a 28-page pamphlet written in Dari and aimed at persuading Afghan troops that deeply insulting behaviours by Western counterparts are typically a result of cultural ignorance, unworthy of blood revenge (Sieff & Leiby 2012). To make an example, the pamphlet included explanations of actions that are normal amongst Westerners, but that can be perceived as profound insults by Afghans:

> As you know, Afghans don't blow their noses in the presence of others. But the practice of blowing your nose in public is a very common practice among the countries where your Coalition partners come from. If a coalition soldier blows his nose in your presence, do not take it as an insult.
>
> (Radio Free Europe/Radio Liberty 2012)

As this case demonstrates, narrowing the cultural gap between foreign troops and local habitants may be the result of small, incremental steps that can greatly contribute to reducing cultural friction leading to violence and resentment amongst the population.

In areas where the erosion of blood revenge gave way to a culture of retaliation, specialised intelligence on local sociocultural practices may offer important insights into how concepts of honour and revenge intersect with political and economic grievances, pushing individuals to join rebel groups during their quest for vengeance. As shown in this chapter, the ideological indoctrination of avengers is often a secondary effect of an initial mobilisation dictated by a perceived humiliation suffered by either the individual himself or society at large. Therefore, a better-informed understanding of sociocultural drivers of violence may provide the conceptual foundations for tailored programmes aimed at preventing and countering violent extremism.

Takeaway no. 2: Use Traditional Conflict Resolution Mechanisms Wisely

Contrary to common misconceptions, retaliatory violence is not the only available way for avengers to restore their honour and avoid social sanctions. In traditional societies, conflicts giving rise to blood revenge are often de-escalated using traditional conflict resolution mechanisms mediated by tribal and clan leaders. When the culprit's family admits guilt and offers to compensate the injured party for the insult or loss received, the latter can rightfully decide to accept the offer, safeguarding its honour without resorting to violence.

For counterinsurgents, paying "blood money" to the relatives of people killed in firefights may sound like an easy, readily available means for offsetting the mobilisation of avengers into the ranks of insurgent groups. Nonetheless, focussing on the monetary component of compensatory forms of conflict resolution fails to capture the true meaning of the institution of "blood money." In traditional societies, where honour is the primary currency and main attribute of social status, people crave respect, *not* money. In fact, monetary compensations are seen as symbols of the culprit's sorrow, and recognition of guilt, for the spilling of blood. Without recognition of guilt, compensation is meaningless. As explained by Howley, a member of a non-governmental organisation working to mediate and solve feuds in post-conflict Bougainville, foreigners often fail to understand what "blood money" is all about:

> To the outsider the gift may seem to be compensation (blood money). However, to most Bougainvilleans compensation (blood money) is repugnant. A gift is to wash away the tears; it in no way is a payment for the loss incurred. Compensation is for gain and is equivalent to setting a value on the life of a loved one. With a gift, one asks for forgiveness; with compensation there is no forgiveness and the person is attempting something which is impossible, that is putting a value on something that cannot be bought or paid for. Not only does the blood money fail to produce reconciliation but it also leads to further disputes and fighting.
>
> (Braithwaite et al. 2010: 73)

In post-Saddam Iraq, for instance, standardised payments of "blood money" to the relatives of people killed in the hostilities were considered satisfactory solely under specific circumstances. As found by Carroll (2015: 50) during interviews with the U.S. veterans and Iraqi sheiks, the kinsmen of individuals killed by the U.S. forces were more likely to renounce blood revenge "when the payments were appropriate and, ideally, not unilaterally set; when the U.S. military took responsibility for the incident; and when the claims process did not dishonour the victim or his or her family."

Instead of attempting to single-handedly solve issues that require complex and lengthy rituals, practitioners would find more luck in empowering traditional authority figures, such as sheiks and tribal leaders, capable of mediating between the two parties and peacefully solve conflicts that would otherwise motivate avengers to seek membership in insurgent bands. In documenting the role played by Australian forces during the post-conflict stabilisation efforts in Bougainville, former senior military advisor and official historian for the Australian army, Bob Breen, argued that the greatest contribution of the peacekeepers was not attempting to solve disputes on their own, but rather "accelerating reconciliations that would have eventually occurred naturally" (Braithwaite et al. 2010: 73, 76). This is the case even for areas where customary codes have eroded. As the authority of tribal or religious leaders often fills the void left by the collapse of state institutions at times of war, avengers adhering to a loose culture of retaliation are typically more inclined to demobilise when traditional conflict resolution mechanisms are made available.

Takeaway no. 3: Be Prepared for the Long Haul

Amidst the chaos of conflict, blood revenge can quickly turn from a highly institutionalised customary code into a loosely defined instrument for restoring individual and collective honour. By relaxing the selectivity principles for a blood revenge killing, the pool of potential targets can grow as wide as to include anyone, fighter or civilian, sharing (sub)ethnic, (sub)religious, or (sub)cultural ties with the perceived culprit. As the conflict drags on and more avengers take part in the hostilities, practices inspired by the culture of retaliation can exacerbate forms of sectarian violence and ethnic conflict, fuelling spirals of escalating retaliatory attacks between the members of different communities. In the ongoing Yemeni Civil War, the unavailability of traditional conflict resolution mechanisms removed all the factors that inhibited the escalatory potential of retaliatory practices. As explained by Brandt,

> The brutalisation of the war was not caused by tribal norms, but rather by their erosion. The ferocity of the battles was of a kind and on a scale exceeding all local rules of engagement, and clearly went far beyond the maximum escalation level of tribal conflict.
>
> (Brandt 2017: 202)

When blood feuds remain unsolved, the simmering potential for intra-communal violence can last indefinitely. In Chechnya, the immense power asymmetry between civilians and security forces has prevented the former from exacting blood revenge against the latter. Nonetheless, the apparent tranquillity of the small republic may conceal a far greater potential for violence. As explained by Souleimanov et al. (2019: 98), "thousands of locals appear to be in the state of postponed blood feud toward Kadyrov, his clan, and his personal army, [the] *Kadyrovtsy*." Similarly, in Iraq, the imprisonment in camps for internally displaced people of thousands of children of killed IS militants created the perfect breeding ground for a new generation of avengers, who will likely seek to retaliate against the Iraqi state for the humiliations suffered in captivity. As explained by an Iraqi government official, there is little doubt that a culture of retaliation is forming amongst the dispossessed youth: "The camps are a time bomb... The fathers are in prison or dead. The mothers are being raped. They will raise the kids accordingly, and their sons will seek revenge" (Taub 2018).

In countries where blood revenge lingers, practitioners ought to consider that successfully stabilising an area affected by insurgent activity or ethnic tensions may not be enough to neutralise the structural grievances that give rise to cycles of intra-communal violence. As a famous Pashtun proverb goes, an oath of blood revenge can be fulfilled even decades after the triggering event: "I took revenge after 100 years, and I took it too soon" (Parker 2009). Accordingly, de-escalating the potential for violence requires a deep engagement with the local communities, including the efforts aimed at empowering traditional authority figures capable of enforcing their decisions on their fellow tribesmen. As indicated in a declassified U.S. government study on the counter-insurgency efforts in Afghanistan, "just placing US and Afghan soldiers at an outpost, conducting token presence patrols, occasionally bantering with locals, and organising a shura once a month are not going to work" (Sexton 2009: 5).

For areas where the remnants of customary codes yielded to unregulated forms of retaliation, a stronger appreciation of local concepts of honour and revenge may reward practitioners with a better understanding of which people are more prone to participate in rebellion to defend their individual or collective honour. Drawing upon evidence collected during interviews with Crimean Tatars who witnessed the 2014 conflict in Eastern Ukraine, Aliyev (2022) found that people living in urban areas, where embeddedness in community life is limited, often eschewed high-risk collective action due to a growing disinterest in customary traditions. As explained by a Crimean Tatar who did not mobilise, "To be a Crimean Tatar nowadays does not mean that you have to blindly obey everything that the elders are saying. Those days are gone! We need to have [our] own brains" (Ibid.: 217). In areas where customary codes are eroding, sociocultural intelligence may assist practitioners in better focussing their efforts and resources, thus reducing the amount of time necessary to de-escalate the potential for violence driven by culturally embedded sociocultural factors.

References

AFP. "Report: Syrian Rebel Defends Gruesome Video as Revenge," *Alarabiya News*, May 14, 2013a. Available at: https://english.alarabiya.net/News/mid dle-east/2013/05/14/Report-Syria-rebel-defends-gruesome-video-as-revenge

AFP. "Rebels Train Syrian Teens to Become 'Killing Machines'," *Alarabiya News*, February 6, 2013b. Available at: https://english.alarabiya.net/articles/2013%2F02%2F06%2F264772

Albertini, Antoine. "La Mia Corsica Violenta," *Le Monde*, Internazionale 1221, September 8, 2017. Available at: www.corsicaoggi.com/sito/wp-content/uploads/2017/09/Internazionale1221.pdf

Aliyev, Huseyn. "Social Sanctions and Violent Mobilization: Lessons from the Crimean Tatar Case," *Post-Soviet Affairs* 38(3), 2022: 206–221. 10.1080/1060586X.2022.2032956

Al-Jabassini, Abdullah. "From Insurgents to Soldiers: The Fifth Assault Corps in Daraa, Southern Syria," *European University Institute*, 2019. 10.2870/742261

Amnesty International. "Bougainville: The Forgotten Human Rights Tragedy," February 26, 1997. Available at: www.amnesty.org/en/documents/asa34/001/1997/en/

Amnesty International. "Papua New Guinea: Human Rights Violations on Bougainville, 1989–1990," February 26, 1990. Available at: www.amnesty.org/en/documents/asa34/005/1990/en/

Associated Press. "Italian Official Quits U.S. Coalition in Iraq," November 18, 2003. Available at: https://eu.heraldtribune.com/story/news/2003/11/18/italian-official-quits-us-coalition-in-iraq/28775441007/

Aubrey, Meg; Aubrey, Rosie; Brodrick, Frances & Brooks, Caroline. "Why Young Syrians Choose to Fight: Vulnerability and Resilience to Recruitment by Violent Extremist Groups in Syria," *International Alert*, May 2016. Available at: www.international-alert.org/publications/why-young-syrians-choose-fight/

Awad, Mokhtar. "Ajnad Misr: The Rise of Homegrown Egyptian Jihadists," *The Tahir Institute for Middle East Policy*, September 18, 2014. Available at: https://timep.org/commentary/analysis/ajnad-misr-rise-homegrown-egyptian-jihadists/

Bar, Shmuel. "The Re-Tribalisation of the Middle East," *Comparative Strategy* 39(2), 128–144. DOI: 10.1080/01495933.2020.1718984.

Baram, Amatzia. "Neo-Tribalism in Iraq: Saddam Hussein's Tribal Policies 1991–1996," *International Journal of Middle East Studies* 29(1), 1997: 1–31. www.jstor.org/stable/163849

Bezham, Frud. "The Deadly Consequences of Cultural Insensitivity in Afghanistan," *Radio Free Europe/Radio Liberty*, September 13, 2012. Available at: www.rferl.org/a/afghanistan-deadly-consequences-of-cultural-insensitiviy/24707511.html

Bhattacharjee, Sumit. "Maoists Kill Two Tribals in Chintapalli," *The Hindu*, July 18, 2019. Available at: www.thehindu.com/news/national/andhra-pradesh/maoists-kill-two-tribals-in-chintapalli/article28535542.ece

Bradshaw, Crystal & Esser, J. Ronald. "The Necessity of Socio-Cultural Intelligence," *NCO Journal*, June 2018. Available at: www.armyupress.army. mil/Portals/7/nco-journal/docs/Socio-Cultural-Intelligence.pdf

Braithwaite, John; Charlesworth, Hilary; Reddy, Peter & Dunn, Leah. *Reconciliation and Architectures of Commitment: Sequencing Peace in Bougainville* (Canberra:Australian National University Press, 2010). ISBN: 9781921666681.

Brandt, Marieke. *Tribes and Politics in Yemen: A History of the Houthi Conflict* (Oxford: Oxford University Press, 2017). ISBN: 9780190911775.

Carnegie, Marc. "Wave of Baghdad Killings as Iraqis Take Revenge on Baath Party," *Lebanon.com*, 22 May, 2003. Available at: www.lebanon.com/news/local/2003/5/22.htm

Carroll, B. Katherine. "The Strangest Tribe: U.S. Military Claims in Iraq," *Middle East Policy* 22(4), 2015: 40–54. https://doi.org/10.1111/mepo.12156

Carroll, B. Katherine. "Tribal Law and Reconciliation in the New Iraq," *Middle East Journal* 65(1), 2011: 11–29.

Coker, Margaret. "Revenge Killings are Soaring in Iraq," *Deseret News*, December 28, 2003. Available at: www.deseret.com/2003/12/28/19803619/revenge-killings-are-soaring-in-iraq

De Carbonnel, Alissa. "Insight - Brutality, Anger Fuel Jihad in Russia's Caucasus," *Thomson Reuters*, August 31, 2012. Available at: www.reuters.com/article/uk-russia-dagestan-idUKBRE87U09U20120831

El-Husseini, Rouba. "Syrian Arab Fighters Battle Daesh Militia for 'Revenge'," *Saudi Gazette*, January 29, 2019. Available at: https://saudigazette.com.sa/article/557995

Elkabir, A. Yassin. "The Study of Urbanization in the Arab World: A Theoretical Perspective," *Ekistics* 50(300), 1983: 232–236. www.jstor.org/stable/43620379

Emmons, Karen. *Adult Wars, Child Soldiers: Voices of Children Involved in Armed Conflict in the East Asia and Pacific Region* (Thailand: UNICEF, 2002). ISBN: 9746850156.

Ezzi, Mazen. "Resurrection of Traditional Leadership Reignites Self-Governance Debate among Druze," *Chatham House*, September 2017. Available at: https://syria.chathamhouse.org/research/resurrection-of-traditional-leadership-reignites-self-governance-debate-among-druze

Fletcher, Martin. "Fighting Back: The City Determined not to Become al Qaeda's Capital," *The Times*, November 20, 2006. Available at: www.thetimes.co.uk/article/fighting-back-the-city-determined-not-to-become-al-qaedas-capital-vg59n2kv3mk

Galal, Rami. "Al-Azhar Works to End Blood Feuds in Egypt," *Al-Monitor*, August 13, 2019. Available at: www.al-monitor.com/pulse/originals/2019/08/egypt-steps-up-efforts-to-stop-blood-feuds.html

Gavriel, J. D. Alexei. "Incorporating Cultural Intelligence into Joint Intelligence: Cultural Intelligence and Ethnographic Intelligence Theory" in *Culture, Conflict, and Counterinsurgency*, edited by Johson, H. Thomas and Zellen, Barry (Stanford: Stanford University Press, 2014), 18–45. ISBN: 9780804785952.

Georgy, Michael. "Iraqi Tribal Revenge Fuels Fallujah's Anti-US Rage," *Reuters*, November 11, 2003. Available at: www.arabnews.com/node/239962

Giglio, Mike & Dickey, Christopher. "In Egypt's Countryside, Vendettas between Police and Islamists Simmer," *Daily Beast*, October 28, 2013. Available at: www.thedailybeast.com/in-egypts-countryside-vendettas-between-police-and-islamists-simmer

Gordon, Robert. "Some Notes Towards Understanding the Dynamics of Blood Money" in *Homicide Compensation in Papua New Guinea: Problems and Prospects*, edited by Richard Scaglion (Papua New Guinea: Office of Information, 1981), 88–102. ISBN: 0724707301.

Hamilton, Douglas & Solomon, Erika. "Syrian Death Squads Darken Picture of Homs Revolt," *Reuters*, December 6, 2011. Available at: www.reuters.com/article/uk-syria-militias-idUKTRE7B51AP20111206

Healy, Jack & Al-Jawoshy, Omar. "As Iraqi Militants Flee, Families are Targets of Blood Reckoning," *The New York Times*, June 5, 2011. Available at: www.nytimes.com/2011/06/05/world/middleeast/05iraq.html

Holmberg, Alana. "It Takes a Village: One Community's Journey toward Peace in Papua New Guinea," *World Bank*, September 30, 2016. Available at: www.worldbank.org/en/news/feature/2016/09/30/it-takes-a-village-one-communitys-journey-toward-peace-in-papua-new-guinea

Human Rights Watch. *"Invisible War:" Russia's Abusive Response to the Dagestan Insurgency* (Human Rights Watch, 2015). ISBN: 978-1-6231-32477.

ICTJ. "'We Didn't Think It Would Hit Us:' Understanding the Impact of Attacks on Schools in Syria," *Save Syrian Schools*, September 2018. Available at: www.ictj.org/sites/default/files/Report_Save_Syrian_Schools_English_Web.pdf

Innes, A. Michael. *Making Sense of Proxy Wars: States, Surrogates & the Use of Force* (Washington: Potomac Books, 2012). ISBN: 978-1-59797-586-5.

International Crisis Group. "Russia's Dagestan: Conflict Causes," Europe Report 192, June 3, 2008. Available at: www.crisisgroup.org/europe-central-asia/caucasus/russianorth-caucasus/russia-s-dagestan-conflict-causes

Ipp, Oren & Cooper, Ilan. "Bougainville Stability Desk Study," *USAID*, 2013. Available at: www.usaid.gov/sites/default/files/documents/1866/Bougainville%20Desk%20Stability%20Study.pdf

Jeffries, Stuart. "Gunmen Fuel Corsican Feuds," *The Guardian*, September 2, 2001. Available at: www.theguardian.com/world/2001/sep/02/stuartjeffries.theobserver

Kagan, Kimberly. "The Anbar Awakening: Displacing Al Qaeda from Its Stronghold in Western Iraq," *The Institute for the Study of War*, March 30, 2007. Available at: www.understandingwar.org/sites/default/files/reports/IraqReport03.pdf

Khalil, Lydia. "Anbar Revenge Brigade Makes Progress in the Fight Against al-Qaeda," *The Jamestown Foundation, Terrorism Focus* 3(12), 2006. Available at: https://jamestown.org/brief/anbar-revenge-brigade-makes-progress-in-the-fight-against-al-qaeda/

Malkasian, Carter. *Illusions of Victory: The Anbar Awakening and the Rise of the Islamic State* (Oxford: Oxford University Press, 2017). ISBN 978–0–19–065942–4.

Maslouh, S. Mohamed. "Categorizing Violence and 'Religions' in the Middle East: Comparison between Narratives of 'Cultural' Violence in Upper Egypt, and 'Religious' Violence in the Middle East," Conference Paper, *Center for Religious Studies*, 2018. Available at: www.academia.edu/download/56925 701/OJR_M_Maslouh.pdf

Montgomery, W. Gary & McWilliams, S. Timothy. *Al-Anbar Awakening: From Insurgency to Counterinsurgency in Iraq, 2004–2009, Volume II, Iraqi Perspectives* (Quantico: Marine Corps University Press, 2009). ISBN-10: 1490405763.

Musaeva, A. G. "Revenge in Dagestan" (original title: Обычай Кровной Мести в Дагестане), *Contemporary Issues of Science and Education* 1, 2015. Available at: https://s.science-education.ru/pdf/2015/1/561.pdf

Nazir, Joseph. "The Tradition of Family Revenge Killings in Upper Egypt," *Connect the Cultures*, September 19, 2016. Available at: www.connectthecultu res.com/revenge-killings-upper-egypt/

Nisbett, E. Richard & Cohen, Dov. *Culture of Honor: The Psychology of Violence in the South* (Boulder: Westview, 1996). ISBN: 0-8133-1992-7.

Parker, K. Brian. "Distinguished Speaker Advises Battalion on Tribal Practices," *U.S. Army*, April 3, 2009. Available at: www.army.mil/article/19222/ distinguished_speaker_advises_battalion_on_tribal_practices

Phillips, Andrew. "The Anbar Awakening: Can It Be Exported to Afghanistan?" *Security Challenges* 5(3), 2009: 27–46. www.jstor.org/stable/26460092

Radio Free Europe/Radio Liberty. "Excerpts from 'Brochure for Understanding the Culture of Coalition Forces'," September 13, 2012. Available at: www. rferl.org/a/excerpts-from-afghan-cultural-sensitivity-guide/24707518.html

Ratelle, Jean-François & Souleimanov, Emil A. "Retaliation in Rebellion: The Missing Link to Explaining Insurgent Violence in Dagestan," *Terrorism and Political Violence* 29(4), 2017: 573–592. DOI: 10.1080/09546553.2015.1005076

Reader, D. H. "Tribalism and Detribalization in Southern and Central Africa," *Zambezia* 1(2), 1970: 55–75. https://hdl.handle.net/10520/AJA03790 622_519

Recknagel, Charles. "Assassination of Daghestan's Sufi Spiritual Leader Raises Specter of New Violence," *Radio Free Europe/Radio Liberty*, August 29, 2012. Available at: www.rferl.org/a/daghestan-sufi-leader-suicide-bombing-/ 24692153.html

Reddy, Peter. "Reconciliation in Bougainville: Civil War, Peacekeeping and Restorative Justice," *Contemporary Justice Review* 11(2), 2008: 117–130. DOI: 10.1080/10282580802057744

Reynolds, A. Michael. "The Northern Caucasus, the Tsarnaevs, and Us," *Foreign Policy Research Institute*, May 2013. Available at: www.files.ethz.ch/isn/166 330/Reynolds_-_Northern_Caucasus.pdf

Rohan, Brian. "In Egypt, Disaffected Youth Increasingly Drawn to Extremism," *AP*, August 4, 2015. Available at: https://apnews.com/548a9a558d9d44f3b 4b1d2530483738c/egypts-disaffected-youth-increasingly-calling-violence

Ronfeldt, David. *In Search of How Societies Work: Tribes—The First and Forever Form* (Santa Monica: RAND Corporation, 2006). Available at: www.rand.org/pubs/working_papers/WR433.html

Sands, Phil. "Tribal Justice Blamed for Deaths of 120 Syrian Police and Soldiers," *The National*, May 17, 2011. Available at: www.thenationalnews.com/world/mena/tribal-justice-blamed-for-deaths-of-120-syrian-police-and-soldiers-1.375373

Schepp, V. Matthias. "Islamists Gain Upper Hand in Russian Republic," *Spiegel International*, July 30, 2010. Available at: www.spiegel.de/international/world/anarchy-in-dagestan-islamists-gain-upper-hand-in-russian-republic-a-709176.html

Sexton, Mark. "How the Taliban Take a Village," *U.S. Army*, Unclassified Document, 2009. Available at: https://publicintelligence.net/ufouo-center-for-army-lessons-learned-how-the-taliban-take-a-village/

Shalabi, Samir. "North Sinai Sawarka Tribe Asks to Fight Alongside Egyptian Army Against Militants," *Egyptian Streets*, December 4, 2017. Available at: https://egyptianstreets.com/2017/12/04/north-sinai-sawarka-tribe-asks-to-fight-alongside-egyptian-army-against-militants/

Sieff, Kevin & Leiby, Richard. "Afghan Troops Get a Lesson in American Cultural Ignorance," *The Washington Post*, September 28, 2012. Available at: www.washingtonpost.com/world/asia_pacific/afghan-troops-get-a-lesson-in-american-cultural-ignorance/2012/09/28/6882621a-08d4-11e2-a10c-fa5a255a9258_story.html

Souleimanov, A. Emil; Abbasov, Namig & Siroky, S. David. "Frankenstein in Grozny: Vertical and Horizontal Cracks in the Foundation of Kadyrov's Rule," *Asia-Europe Journal* 17, 2019: 87–103. https://doi.org/10.1007/s10308-018-0520-y

Souleimanov, A. Emil & Aliyev, Huseyn. *The Individual Disengagement of Avengers, Nationalists, and Jihadists: Why Ex-militants Choose to Abandon Violence in the North Caucasus* (Basingstoke: Palgrave Macmillan, 2014). ISBN: 978-1-349-50528-9.

Tampa Bay Times. "U.S. Swaps Blood Money for Peace in Iraqi City," July 31, 2003. Available at: www.tampabay.com/archive/2003/07/31/u-s-swaps-blood-money-for-peace-in-iraqi-city/

Taub, Ben. "Iraq's Post-ISIS Campaign of Revenge," *The New Yorker*, December 17, 2018. Available at: www.newyorker.com/magazine/2018/12/24/iraqs-post-isis-campaign-of-revenge

The Moscow Times. "5 Men Found Shot to Death in Forest in Russia's Dagestan," September 20, 2015. Available at: www.themoscowtimes.com/2015/09/20/tatar-activists-block-roads-into-russia-annexed-crimea-a49679

United Nations. "UN Official Says with Autonomous Government in Place in Bougainville, UN Mandate Complete," July 6, 2005. Available at: https://news.un.org/en/story/2005/07/143972-un-official-says-autonomous-government-place-bougainville-un-mandate-complete

Vatchagaev, Mairbek. "Dagestani Anti-Insurgency Vigilante Group Posts Internet Video," *The Jamestown Foundation, Eurasia Daily Monitor* 9(133), July 13, 2012.

Available at: https://jamestown.org/program/dagestani-anti-insurgency-vigilante-group-posts-internet-video-2/

Verma, Gargi. "Dantewada: Maoists Kill Brother of Rebel Who Became Cop," *Indian Express*, January 15, 2020. Available at: https://indianexpress.com/article/india/dantewada-maoists-kill-brother-of-rebel-who-became-cop-6216877/

6 Conclusion

Considered "the most prevalent form of conflict" since the second half of the 20th century, irregular warfare has seen some of its longest and bloodiest manifestations in areas, such as Afghanistan, Chechnya, Iraq, and Syria, where customary codes are deeply embedded within the local sociocultural milieu (Beckett 2005: 1). Yet, scholars of security studies have largely left unexplored the ways in which sociocultural codes shape the dynamics of civil wars and insurgencies. Addressing the dearth of cross-case research in the sociocultural aspects of irregular warfare, this book offered an in-depth analysis of how blood revenge manifests itself during the inception, course, and aftermath of armed conflicts.

To provide an accurate assessment of the ways in which blood revenge and its modern remnants shape the dynamics of irregular conflicts, the book first discussed the attributes of blood revenge and the mechanisms engendering its decline. Anchoring its arguments in a large body of anthropological, ethnographic, and historical research, the book showed that blood revenge erodes following the manifestation of four interrelated mechanisms, defined in Chapter 3 as the centralisation of the state's judicial apparatus, the penalisation of self-made justice, the decline of the culture of honour, and the collective stigmatisation of revenge as a socially acceptable response to interpersonal conflicts.

For blood revenge to disappear, a society must undergo both processes of state centralisation and societal rejection of kinship-centred collective punishment. While the interruption of the former engenders a resurgence of blood revenge in cultures of honour, as in post-Communism Albania, Iraq in the mid-2000s, and Egypt following the 2011 Arab uprisings, the lack of the latter breeds a culture of retaliation based on remnants of customary codes centred on honour and revenge. Where the process of state centralisation is successful, but society does not relinquish traditional values, blood revenge is likely to outlast the authority's suppressive efforts. To sum up, the processes leading to the erosion of blood revenge are

DOI: 10.4324/9781003387527-6

complex and sensitive to events such as conflicts, political instability, and social unrest. Much can go wrong, and when the processes are interrupted the potential for a resurgence in revenge killings is heightened.

In cultures where men are expected to avenge deaths, injuries, or insults suffered by one or more kinsmen, blood revenge alters the baseline dynamics of irregular conflicts, changing the key patterns of violent mobilisation, target selection, recruitment, and disengagement from violence. First, avengers are compelled to join armed groups and participate in high-risk combat operations to maximise their chances of exacting vengeance against their blood enemies. While conventional wisdom points to ideological, political, religious, or economic considerations as the key triggers of violent mobilisation, avengers are typically drawn to violence by *apolitical* motives and *irrespective* of any individual or collective pay-off associated with taking part in armed hostilities.

Second, avengers may not be able to target the direct culprit or one of his close male agnates. To overcome the lack of information or capabilities and still perform a blood revenge killing, avengers may decide to extend the pool of viable targets to encompass the culprit's comrades-in-arms, any member of the related armed group, down to any individual belonging to (sub)ethnic, (sub)religious, or (sub)cultural groups sharing a connection with the preferred—yet unreachable—target. The broadening of the list of potential targets exposes thousands of civilians to the risk of being targeted by avengers, who contribute to driving cycles of tit-for-tat revenge killings between ethnically, religiously, or culturally distant groups.

Third, armed groups may take advantage of the situation, offering support to avengers in return for their participation in the hostilities. Each warring side can thus recruit and retain a pool of highly motivated members, unlikely to demobilise or defect due to the risks run by relatives of fighters involved in blood feuds with members of rival groups. Armed actors may even turn blood revenge into an effective counter-defection mechanism, holding the recruits' relatives as hostages of retaliatory raids should attempts of defection or mutiny be made. Once recruited by an armed faction, avengers are often left with no choice other than keep fighting to shield their family members from the threat of blood revenge attacks.

In areas where the processes of state centralisation and societal modernisation have not yet eroded tribal customary laws, blood revenge survives and can resurge during periods of political instability. Conversely, the erosion of blood revenge does not necessarily entail an utter disappearance of retaliatory practices. In societies where concepts of male honour and warrior ethos endure, insults and humiliations may still prompt avengers to take up arms and "get even" with the perpetrators. No longer bound to the tightly regulated principles of blood revenge, individuals are left free to decide whether a perceived insult or humiliation calls for a retaliatory response. Accordingly, the triggers of violent mobilisation increase in scope and character, adding religious, ideological, and economic motives atop the apolitical drivers of institutionalised forms of blood revenge. The dissolution of the selectivity principles of blood revenge adds fuel to the fire, with avengers widening the pool of potential targets in accordance with their own interpretation of individual and collective guilt. While striking against the relatives of direct culprits may no longer be considered as a socially acceptable practice due to the weakening of kinship ties, avengers may still decide to retaliate against anyone associated with the "guilty" community, which may encompass entire (sub)ethnic, (sub)religious, or (sub)cultural communities. For armed actors, the presence of a culture of retaliation offers the opportunity to attract and retain individuals willing to take part in high-risk collective action, similarly to insurgent groups and pro-government militias operating in areas where blood revenge endures. In short, even in countries where customary codes withered away, the baseline logic of blood revenge survives and may flare up again at times of war and political instability. Under the pressure of modernisation processes, blood revenge dissolves and assumes new forms, largely unregulated and less widespread, but still practised. This explains why, in irregular conflicts taking place in areas where concepts of honour and revenge linger, episodes of retributive violence may register a spike after years, if not decades, of a relative lull.

These findings bear important implications for the community of irregular warfare professionals. Although the involvement of Western forces in military operations across the globe elevated the role of cultural intelligence to a key component of the strategic toolkit in use amongst counter-insurgents, the wealth of information made available is often unfocused or unrelated to the specific challenges faced by practitioners on the ground. As explained by retired U.S. Colonel Spracher, practitioners are in constant need of actionable, high-quality intelligence on the complexity of specific foreign cultural environments: "The role of [cultural] intelligence is clear here. We need more of it, and we need more of the right kind of it" (Spracher 2012: 114). Diving deep into the largely overlooked role of blood revenge in irregular conflicts, this book showed that cultural intelligence offers valuable insights to better prevent and counter the threat of insurgent violence. In areas where concepts of honour and revenge are prominent, building connections with tribal authorities capable of keeping their fellow tribesmen in check is far more effective than relying on "monetary ammunition," under the faulty assumption that economic benefits may suffice in persuading people to refrain from violence. Where blood revenge gave way to a culture of retaliation, specialised intelligence may disclose how cultural drivers of violence intersect with political, religious, and economic grievances, thus shedding light on the leverages used by insurgent actors to attract and radicalise new recruits. A stronger understanding of the cultural drivers of violence offers, in turn, better chances of being successful at de-escalating conflicts and preventing violent extremism through traditional conflict resolution mechanisms.

Despite a growing appetite for cultural intelligence amongst decision-makers and military practitioners, scholars of security studies have only marginally explored the ways in which sociocultural codes shape the micro-dynamics of irregular conflicts, and how cultural drivers of violence impact the broader evolution of armed hostilities. As explained by Balcells and Justino (2014: 1345), the literature on the micro-dynamics of violence in civil wars and insurgencies "has yet to consider specific linkages between micro-level conflict dynamics and wider political, economic, and social processes." In focussing on how blood revenge and its unregulated variants shape irregular conflicts, this book contributed to build up the groundwork necessary to bridge the micro-level analysis of insurgent violence with the research supporting macro-level explanations of global armed conflicts. One way for scholars of security studies to further advance this stream of research is through a more sustained interaction with other fields of studies, especially anthropology, ethnography, and sociology. As several aspects of the cultural domain of irregular warfare remain underexplored, new cross-case interdisciplinary research may offer key leads on how to further strengthen the collective understanding of violence in armed conflicts.

This book argued, and empirically demonstrated, that blood revenge plays an important role in shaping the character of violence in irregular conflicts, even in areas where its institutionalised form has given way to unregulated retaliatory practices resting upon cultural concepts of honour and revenge. Nonetheless, practitioners involved in counter-insurgency, stability, and peacekeeping operations continue to underestimate and—at times—misapprehend the phenomenon. Further research is warranted to enrich the current understanding of the social, political, and military challenges posed by the lingering presence of blood revenge in theatres of irregular conflicts.

References

Balcells, Laia & Justino, Patricia. "Bridging Micro and Macro Approaches on Civil Wars and Political Violence: Issues, Challenges, and the Way Forward," *The Journal of Conflict Resolution* 58(8), 2014: 1343–1359. www.jstor.org/sta ble/24546207

Beckett, F. W. Ian. *Insurgency in Iraq: An Historical Perspective* (Carlisle: Strategic Studies Institute, U.S. Army War College, January 2005). ISBN 1-58487-183-0.

Spracher, C. William. "Seeking Cultural Intelligence in the Desert's Shifting Sands While Keeping Peace Along the Berm," *American Intelligence Journal* 30(1), 2012: 105–115. www.jstor.org/stable/10.2307/26201991

Index

For Product Safety Concerns and Information please contact our EU
representative GPSR@taylorandfrancis.com
Taylor & Francis Verlag GmbH, Kaufingerstraße 24, 80331 München, Germany

www.ingramcontent.com/pod-product-compliance
Lightning Source LLC
Chambersburg PA
CBHW071054280326
41928CB00050B/2505

* 9 7 8 1 0 3 2 4 8 1 2 4 1 *